The Complete Guide
to
Prize Contests,
Sweepstakes,
and
How to Win Them

The Complete Guide to Prize Contests, Sweepstakes, and How to Win Them

by
SELMA GLASSER

FREDERICK FELL PUBLISHERS, Inc.   *   New York, New York

ISBN 0-8119-0327-3

For information address:

Frederick Fell Publishers, Inc.
386 Park Avenue South
New York, New York 10016

MANUFACTURED IN THE UNITED STATES OF AMERICA

1 2 3 4 5 6 7 8 9 0

*Dedicated to
my most precious prizes—
my children.*

PREFACE

Welcome to the wonderful world of INSTANT INCOME, IN-STANT BYLINES, and INSTANT FUN! We are immersed in a fast-paced world of hurry-go-round times—instant coffee, instant cameras, and countless instant pleasures. It is fitting that the contents of this book provide the necessary ingredients for winning the satisfying and gratifying INSTANT extras every creative person craves.

One day you may wear a cloth coat, the next day mink! You worry about your lack of funds for your next vacation, and presto, there's an expensive trip for two to some exotic resort awarded to you, right out of the blue! Your house may be heated with oil today, but tomorrow's prize may provide a complete gas heat installation in your home! You search for carfare in your pocket one day, and the next day you find car keys there, for the brand new car you just won! Or you may dream of becoming a highly-paid copywriter, columnist, or writer of features for magazines or newspapers, and know-how and show-how revealed in these pages may help you achieve these goals!

If you seek personal fulfillment, writing recognition, and higher earnings for your creative endeavors, innumerable opportunities await! Provided you are equipped with an intense desire to succeed and have some interest in writing, and also have those qualities without which any ability cannot emerge—purpose, perseverance, and adaptability—then *The Complete Guide to Prize Contests, Sweepstakes, and How to Win Them* is the key to unlock those doors of success and achievement. You can become a Rembrandt in the art of winning, or you can stay at the paint-by-number stage. How well you study and utilize the contents of this volume is the determining factor.

The dictionary is the only place where success comes before work, and you can't make dollars by depositing your quarters in an easy chair. Add to that, some succinct quotes from Shakespeare:

"Speak, breathe, discuss; brief, short, quick, snap."—*The Merry Wives of Windsor*. Or, "Brevity is the soul of wit."—*Hamlet*.

Therein is the message of this book. While the chapters in this volume are aimed specifically at winning prize contests, the formulas outlined can be applied equally well to all forms of verbal expression—from ad writing to article writing to public speaking and so on—for INSTANT INCOME.

New coined words emerge. Witness "gasohol" (a combination of gasoline and alcohol), "palimony" (a term to describe Michelle Triola's cash settlement from actor Lee Marvin), "galimony" (an oil heiress's divorce payoff to her estranged, nonworking husband), and finally "gallimony" (The *New York Daily News'* editorial comment on the latter case). (See Chapter 9, How to Win Name Contests.)

Witness also Rex Reed's description of Jacqueline Bisset: "The *shallow* roles into *tanks* of public attention." In another column he describes the movie *An Unmarried Woman:* "the *tempo* of New York—behind the *ticking* reality of *time* measured by an *Accutron* sign."

Liz Smith quotes car king Steve Kessler: "When it comes to cities the Big *Apple* is still Top *Banana*."

Irwin Shaw was quoted in *Writer's Digest:* "Writing is an intellectual *contact sport,* similar in some respects to *football*. The effort required can be exhausting, the *goal* reached, and you are hurt on almost every *play* but that doesn't deprive a man or boy from getting peculiar pleasures from the *game*."

Pete Hamill once described a sidewalk incident: "Yesterday, before the *actors* in the Crown Heights *drama* had taken the afternoon *stage* . . ."

Louis Rukeyser, in a column that he called "You're *Sick, Sick, Sick; Get Well* First," starts an open letter to an inflation fighter thus: "Run, don't walk to your *doctor* without delay. You are *coming down with* a particularly *virulent case of Potomac fever*." He goes on to describe "*the dread disease*" in terms of "*delirious* ramblings"—"*symptoms*"—"*get help*"—"*caught the bug*"—and ends up with "*get help fast*."

Robert Perry called a column on gardening "Your Yard is a *Canvas;* Prepare it Now for a Summer *Masterpiece*."

In the movie *Manhattan,* which stars Woody Allen, the relationship between 42-year-old Allen and 17-year-old Mariel Hemingway is intriguing. He tells her, "Just think of me as a *detour* on the *highway* of life." Isn't that a perfect use of an analogy on transportation? (See chapter 12 in this book, also pages 30 to 31 in *Analogy Anthology*.)

Myrna Blyth, in an article for *Family Circle* entitled "The Wise Woman of Waikiki," asks 76-year-old Clare Booth Luce, "Do you find aging difficult?" Ms. Luce's answer is a perfect example of an analogy on naval terminology. (See pages 24 to 25 of *Analogy Anthology* or Chapter 12 of this book.) Ms. Luce's answer was: "It's a *shipwreck.* One thing after another goes *overboard.* I seem to have lost my *starboard* and *port lights.* I think I still have my *compass.* The *rudder's* still all right but the *boiler room's* in a shocking state! And there again, if old age is a *shipwreck* for everyone, those who have money can be *shipwrecked* on a *pleasant beach* rather than *on the rocks,* beaten by the *storms.*"

All the above examples relate to chapter 12, Analogy in Action.

Ad writers employ contest-writing techniques. The Promenade Cafe in Rockefeller Plaza describes its skaters' place thus: "Eat, *Rink* and Be Merry." Consider the following: Mitch Parrish's "The Last Time I Heard *Parrish*"; or Rit's "When You're *Dyeing* for a Change" or Sanyo's "Electric shavers *draw interest* in their *shavings bank*"; or Gerald Nachman's column called "*Rice* Guys Finish First"; or Ruth Rosenbaum's "Air *Fare*" about airline food; or Nathan's introduction to its Chick-A-Bun "There's Something New Under the *Bun.*" Wouldn't you consider them serious contenders to the contents of this book and its teachings? Add to these, The Cattleman Restaurant's slogan on radio: "Where you can get your *steak rare* and entertainment *well done.*"

Ideas for such clever ads, captions, and slogans can be gleaned from the chapters How to Win Caption Contests and How to Win Slogan Contests.

An enterprising chiropractor, Dr. David Koffman, has written a song he calls "The Spine Song" which greets customers on the telephone with this advertising jingle: "Spine, spine, spine; I hope that yours is fine; This song's about some bones, it's true; they're found inside each one of you." This release came out on Koffman's "Slipped Disc Label." This doctor rhymes well, and his puns and parodies are ingeniously expressed. Readers of this book might pick up pertinent pointers on the subject from the chapter Rhyme, Rhythm, and Reason.

All the prizewinning techniques illustrated in these samples of skillful writing are incorporated in this winning volume of THE COMPLETE GUIDE TO PRIZE CONTESTS, SWEEPSTAKES, AND HOW TO WIN THEM. Read it and reap!

FOREWORD

This book has only one purpose—to help the reader earn IN-STANT INCOME. With the aid of pen, paper, and, perhaps, a typewriter, anyone can win fabulous prizes in creative contests that call for skillful use of words, or in sweepstakes that require nothing more than filling out the entry form; or you can earn cash for writing by using the contest-winning techniques included herein.

Columnists, educators, presidents, and all kinds of intellectuals employ many of the secrets revealed here in their speeches, papers, and enterprises. Therefore, this book serves not only prize pursuers, but also provides invaluable aid to all who delve into the written or spoken word.

The author has assembled in this volume every practical aid available for the composition of prizeworthy entries in the most popular contest classifications, as specified in separate chapters covering each major category.

While this book is intended primarily to bring winning assistance to those who have had little or no success so far in their pursuit of contest prizes, even experienced followers of the contest hobby should find much of value in these pages, especially in reviewing various techniques from which new winning ideas and approaches may be derived.

Readers who are unfamiliar with contest terminology are advised to consult the Glossary at the back of this book whenever they encounter any word that may have a special meaning in this field.

Some of the entry examples presented here for your guidance came from the author's own files; others are from the "Sources of Success," fully described in Chapter 13; many are from friends as well as prizewinning students throughout the country and at Brooklyn College (where the author teaches a course entitled "Writing for Prize & Publication").

All entries were created by capable contestants who have generously allowed their winning material to be made public through media serving the needs of all prize seekers.

To such warmhearted winners, who have given so freely of their own knowledge to benefit others striving for similar awards, the author extends her profound gratitude—while hoping that every reader of this book will have good reason to share that feeling soon.

SELMA GLASSER

CONTENTS

The Complete Guide
to
Prize Contests,
Sweepstakes,
and
How to Win Them

Chapter 1

CONTESTDOM—REALM OF RICH REWARDS

Contestdom is a wonderful world where ordinary people can enjoy extraordinary fortune, in events like these:

For completing a two-line jingle about a popular brand of soap, a Texas insurance man was offered his choice of $25,000 in cash or the full income from a producing oil well. He took the lump sum award.

For telling why she wanted to own a combination washing and drying machine, a Missouri housewife won her weight in gold. At $35 an ounce, the rate at that time, her prize amounted to a plump $50,318.

For describing what she liked about a new model car, in 25 words, a young Minnesota bride won $500 a month for life. With her normal life expectancy, that award may eventually total as much as $330,000—which would be an all-time high for any creative contest prize.

Winning Secrets to Be Revealed

In a later chapter, you'll find out more about these fortunate folks and others who have won fabulous contest prizes. Right now, you may be wondering whether such exciting events can happen to YOU as well. They can, indeed—if you learn how to apply the Secrets of Winning that are revealed in this book.

You will find here scores of entries that have actually won prizes in the most popular kinds of contests—statements, slogans, jingles, limericks, names, titles, and captions.

There is no better way to learn how to write winning entries than to study successful examples of such work—and you will find them in the following chapters, arranged for ready reference to assist your efforts in current contests.

First, however, let's survey contestdom as a whole, to get an idea of its size, scope, and structure, so that you can better understand how knowledgeable participation in this field may make your fondest dreams come true.

Years of Contests

We can look back on years of prize give-aways in the United States since 1900. Of course, there had been some contests—more literary than commercial—in this country before the present century began, but they were too rare to be recorded here. Even in 1900, contesting was a comparatively unknown hobby, with few followers and with awards amounting to only $15,000.

By 1910, newspaper files show that $500,000 in prizes were offered, and there were about 100,000 contest fans. Within ten years, the number of prize-seekers had grown to a million, mostly attracted by newspaper and magazine contests.

By 1930, national commercial advertisers had become convinced that prize contests offered a fertile field for promoting the sales of their products. During that decade, their ever-increasing offers of cash and merchandise brought the number of entrants to nearly 12 million, and the total value of prizes for the ten-year span soared past the $100-million mark.

The Big Awards Begin

Some outstanding contests of that period are worth special mention:

In 1933, *The American Weekly* awarded $1,200 a year for life to William C. Gamble of Fairfield, Conn., for his slogan, "The Nation's Reading Habit," which was used for many years by that publication.

In 1935, the biggest prize contest ever staged until that time was conducted by Seminole Tissues. It offered $125,000 in merchandise, including 100 automobiles, for the best slogans written on Seminole wrappers. This contest attracted a total of 3,264,325 entries.

Also in 1935, Camay awarded $1,000 a year for life to Miss Helen Duncan of Chicago for her first-prize letter; and Colgate-Palmolive-Peet created a national sensation with its offer of 20 free tours of Europe for the best entries on "Why I Use and Prefer Palmolive Soap."

In the early 1940's, during World War II, most all contests diminished in size and quantity; but after the war was over, they came back in greater numbers than ever, offering fabulous prizes in profusion.

When the war ended, right up to the time this book was written, every single year has seen scores of huge prize contests, of which the following annual examples are typical.

Some Notable Contests

- —Pepsodent offered $30,000 for finishing a statement.
- —*Magazine Digest* offered $10,000 for jokes.
- —Borden offered $20,000 for naming a calf.
- —Chiffon Flakes offered 30 automobiles and $45,000 in cash for a two-line jingle.
- —Colgate offered $100,000 for finishing a statement.
- —Kaiser-Frazer offered $50,000 for naming a new car.
- —Lipton offered $70,000 for limerick last lines.
- —General Mills offered $100 a month for life and $250,000 in other prizes for finishing a statement.
- —Monarch Foods offered prizes worth $100,000 for last lines to their limerick's.
- —Dial Soap offered $75,000 for finishing a two-line jingle.
- —Chevrolet offered prizes worth $330,000 for finishing a statement.
- —American Motors offered $250,000 for naming a car body.
- —Mercury offered prizes worth $450,000 for last lines to a jingle.
- —Plymouth offered $500 a month for life and 18 cars for finishing a statement.
- —General Foods offered $100,000 for naming cakes.
- —Gulf Oil offered prizes worth $500,000 for finishing a statement.
- —Lever Brothers offered *a million dollars in prizes* for last lines to a jingle.
- —Columbia Records offered $100,000 for finishing a statement.
- —Proctor & Gamble offered $50,000 for naming a character in an ad.
- —Currently, fabulous trips all over the world, tours of the U.S., scholarship grants, dream kitchens, major appliances, and tremendous cash prizes are being awarded, such as Bic's $50,000 "Flick My Bic" lime rick contest and Pillsbury's $100,000 Bake-Off® contest.

21

Why Contests Will Continue

A reliable survey has shown that at present, at least 20,000,000 Americans enter commercial contests every year, submitting approximately 45,000,000 entries annually.

Barring any major upset to our national economy, contests will assuredly continue to offer an endless flow of lavish awards for many years to come.

There are two sound reasons for this assurance. One is past performance, and the other, public preference. Any business-promoting method that has proved profitable—as contests have—for so many years will not be abandoned in the foreseeable future.

Sweepstake contests, which entail little writing ability or particular aptitude for participation, are another form of competition. They are covered completely in Chapter 18. Although they seem to be popular at the present time, sweepstakes have never managed to displace write-in contests from public favor or the sponsor's. Why? Simply because the entrants enjoy working on a contest which involves the pleasure of creating something all their own—a name, slogan, jingle, or statement. From the sponsor's point of view, a real write-in competition usually requires a genuine box top or label from a product, and therefore, sells the sponsor's wares. In a sweepstakes, writing the name of the product in block letters is often the only requirement, since it is illegal to demand a purchase in this type of contest.

The Best Is Yet to Come

National manufacturers and their advertising agencies are well aware of this popular fondness for creative contests. Coupled with their long record of proven success in stimulating sales, no further reasons are needed to ensure the continued sponsorship of such contests by most of the richest industries in this country.

As business booms and new products appear on the market, sales-promoting prize contests will grow in profusion and prodigality. Even the biggest offers of past years will be surpassed as sponsors vie for the fickle favor of the buying public.

Is There a Fortune in Your Future?

You can share in the fortunes to be given away in the near future by learning *now*, through this book, how to win contest prizes in the same way that others have won major awards in past contests.

Don't be daunted by the thought that you may be competing against millions of other entrants for some desirable prizes. Remember that the vast multitude of contestants submit their entries in hit-or-miss fashion, relying solely on their own vague, random, and often poorly-expressed ideas, without the aid of a guide book like this one.

Comparatively few entrants possess the winning knowledge that will be divulged here. Once you have mastered these Techniques for Triumph, you will possess a tremendous advantage over your untrained competitors—an advantage which could lead to a fortune in your future!

Chapter 2

WINNOWING THE WINNERS

Most people who enter contests give very little thought, if any, to the actual treatment their work will get on the receiving end. They may devote a lot of time and effort to composing the best entries they can, then daydream about enjoying expected awards; but they have only a hazy idea of what really happens to their submission after it has been dropped in the mail box.

Is such information important to you, as a would-be winner? Indeed, it is—for a thorough understanding of this phase of contesting will help you compose, prepare, and submit your entries so that they will have a maximim chance to win.

How Contests Are Judged

If you are an average contest trier—with no inside knowledge of this popular pastime—you may think that your entry will go directly to the attention of the contest sponsor, who will examine it personally along with all others submitted, select the best ones, and announce the winners.

Such is not the case. Sponsors rarely see the entries sent to their contests. The entire operation of all major prize promotions is handled from beginning to end by professional judging agencies, hired expressly for that work by the sponsor. Their procedure is virtually the same for every big national contest.

First, all entries are picked up in mail sacks—sometimes filling several trucks—at the post office to which they were addressed. Delivered to the judging headquarters, the letters are passed through envelope-slitting machines and the contents removed by clerks whose main duty is to check them for "qualifiers"—meaning the box top, label, or wrapper required as proof that the entrant purchased the contest product.

What Happens to Rule Breakers

Entries lacking qualifiers are thrown out without further consideration. Illegible submissions meet the same fate, as do those which were postmarked after the contest's closing date.

The rest of the entries are then checked for other violatons, such as exceeding the number of words allowed, omitting entrant's name and address, failing to include dealer's name and address (if that was called for), or writing instead of printing, as rules may specify.

When all rule breakers are discarded—and they often amount to 40 percent of the total submitted—eligible entries are turned over to a staff of preliminary readers. Their job is to eliminate obviously unfit entries—those which are senseless, incomprehensible, profane, or obscene.

At the same time, decorated entries are stripped of all embellishments or copied on plain paper, since "fancy" entries are not favored by any national contest judging agency.

Prize Winners Are Picked by Points

After this come the junior judges, who rate the remaining entries according to aptness, sincerity, originality, and—in the case of jingle contests—correct rhyming. Here duplication gets in its deadly work, as thousands of entries are tossed out because they sound too much alike.

Next, the surviving entries—now greatly reduced in number—reach the senior judges, who score each one by points on such elements as relevancy, concreteness, clarity, readability, uniqueness, or other special factors required by the contest under consideration.

Finally, all graded entries are reviewed by a tribunal of agency executives, who select the winning entries according to their point rating, from the highest to the lowest. The list of chosen winners is then relayed to the contest sponsor, who will eventually pay out the prizes in the order stipulated by his hired judges.

Exactness Is Important

Now, you may wonder, in what way can familiarity with the foregoing facts help you to win? To understand that fully, you must consider each contest processing procedure in relation to your own composition, preparation, and submission of entries.

First, be sure that the envelope containing your entry is addressed *exactly* as directed in the contest ad or entry blank. Suppose the announced address appears like this:

> Brown Brothers, Dept. C.
> P.O. Box 798
> New York, N.Y. 10046

Don't abbreviate "Brothers" as "Bros." Don't omit "P.O." and don't write it out as "Post Office." Make certain you have the box number correct—not 789. Don't leave out the zip code 10046. And be sure to include "Dept. C." It may seem meaningless to you; but it indicates what source prompted your entry—for example, "C" may represent the magazine *Cosmopolitan*—so that the sponsor can ultimately learn which ads drew the greatest response.

If your address varies in *any* way from the given one, you may be disqualified before your envelope is even opened. However, if the same contest uses different forms of address in various advertisements, you may safely use any one of them exactly as announced.

Hints to Heed

Having been properly addressed, your letter has passed the first hurdle. It now faces the mechanical mail opener. This is a fast-operating machine which slits envelope tops after the contents have been jogged down to the bottom. If an envelope is stuffed too tightly, part of its contents will be sliced off by the opening machine. To avoid any such damage to your entry, just be sure it is folded to allow some extra space—at least one-quarter inch—within the envelope.

Since most contests have definite closing dates by which entries must be mailed, any submission bearing a later postmark—even a single day—will be discarded unread. So be sure to mail your entries before the announced deadline.

Of course, entries that are so poorly written as to be unreadable cannot be considered. Type your entries if possible; or write them clearly, in ink. Never use pencil. If your handwriting is not easily understood and you have no typewriter, you'd do well to print your entire entry as plainly as possible.

Box Tops, Blanks, and Word Limits

Now comes the essential matter of qualifiers. Almost all commercial contests require you to send "proof of purchase" with your entry—meaning the box top, label, or wrapper from the sponsor's product. When rules require any such qualifier, you *must* include it—your entry will not have the slightest chance of getting past the first mail checker, no matter how good your work may be.

The same stringent rule applies to official entry blanks and to special contest forms. When required, they must be used. However, if the rules allow a choice between blanks or any plain paper, you needn't hesitate to employ your own stationery.

Exceeding the given word limit is another rule violation that eliminates many entries. If you are told to finish a sentence in 25 words or less, don't go over that allowance *by even a single word* or your entry will be disqualified. Count every word carefully; and, to play safe, you should consider as two words such contractions as "don't," "she's," "they've," etc. However, it is quite permissible to use *less* than the maximum number of words allowed.

In addition to your own name and address on each separate entry which you submit, some contests ask for the name and address of your dealer. If requested, such information must be given.

No Decoration Needed

When entering *national* contests, do not bother to decorate your entries or prepare them in any elaborate or fancy manner. Such presentation will prove of no benefit at all, though it will not actually cause your entry to be discarded. Any embellishment will simply be removed in the preliminary processing stages. Whatever value decoration may have in *local* contests will be discussed in a later chapter.

To sum up these negative regulations: your entry must not lack anything required by the rules if it is to remain in the running. To express the same thought in a positive way, you have to obey every stated condition for eligibility. Nonconformists will get nowhere in contestdom.

Factors That Win Favor

Suppose, then, that your entry has faithfully followed all stipulations and has succeeded in passing the preliminary readers. It now proceeds to the junior judges for consideration of whatever merits it may possess.

Current judging standards are based on a point system, with a

27

maximum percentage of points allotted to each of several factors. Junior contest judges may use a rating chart with the following typical values:

1. Aptness 25%
2. Sincerity 25%
3. Clarity 20%
4. Originality 30%

To make your entries rate high on these four factors, you must understand the full meaning of each term. While their significance may vary somewhat in relation to the product being described, this analysis will hold true for most statement contests. Other types of contests are covered elsewhere in this book.

APTNESS

To be apt or appropriate, your composition must fit the specific subject. Suppose you are describing a product called "Swell Frosting Mix." It is not enough to say that this mix makes a delicious cake topping. While that may be true, it is much too vague. You must be more definite. For example, you might say Swell Frosting Mix is so smooth and creamy that it never hardens before your cake is consumed, even if left over a few days.

SINCERITY

To be sincere, your statement must be believable. Don't make wild, exaggerated claims for the product. Don't say it's better than any other brand on the market. The judges will doubt whether you've actually tested all other brands or whether you're qualified to make such a sweeping statement. Instead, you might say that Swell is the only frosting you've ever tried that pleases every member of your family, from Grandpa to Junior. That sounds earnest and reasonable. The judges can believe you; and they'll consider your entry sincere.

CLARITY

To achieve clarity, the meaning of your words must be so clear that they can be easily understood at first reading. Busy judges have neither the time nor the inclination to fathom entries which are in any way difficult to comprehend. Don't employ figures of speech that are too fancy or far-fetched, like calling the frosting product "ethereal as eiderdown." Use simple yet distinctive language. You could say that Swell Mix makes a "fluffy" frosting rather than a "light" one. Why? Because the word "fluffy" brings a definite image to the reader's mind of a delicately creamy cake coating, while the word "light" does not create any such clear mental picture. If you understand that difference, you know what "clarity" means.

ORIGINALITY

To write with originality, you must avoid the obvious. Don't submit the first expression that pops into your head. Thousands of other entrants will probably get the same idea: For example, when writing about a frosting, most people think of it as something that covers the upper surface of a cake; and that thought will lead them to say it's "TOPS for taste." After seeing this identical phrase repeated over and over by a multitude of entrants, the word-weary judges will simply throw out all entries containing that trite expression—and who can blame them for doing so? Therefore, you must strive to say something *different* about a product—something that will stand out from most of the other commonplace or repetitious entries. In later chapters, you will learn exactly how originality can be achieved.

Further Factors to Be Considered

After the junior judges have eliminated all submissions that failed to score a certain number of "passing points" on the rating chart, the surviving entries go through the semi-final and final phases described earlier in this chapter.

Since these ultimate judgments—which decide the actual order of winners—are based on varying standards according to the type of competition under consideration, these factors will be fully discussed in the chapters on jingles, slogans, statements, and other specific contest subjects.

Chapter 3

RHYME, RHYTHM, AND REASON

You need no inborn poetic talent to win commercial contests based on rhymes. Even if you have never written a single stanza before, you can learn all requirements for composing versified entries from this chapter and the ones following, covering the basic forms of popular rhyming contests.

In the wide field of "true" poetry, there are many variations of lyrical expression—sonnets, rondeaus, ballads, odes, and other rather complicated patterns. Commercial verse, as used in most contests, also follows definite styles of rhyming; but their nature is relatively simple and easy to understand.

Three Main Types of Contest Verse

Contest rhymes fall into three major classifications:

1. Couplets
2. Quatrains
3. Limericks

All three types are generally known as "jingles," but each has its distinctive characteristics, which you should clearly recognize and understand.

THE COUPLET

A couplet consists of only two lines which rhyme with each other, as in this example:

> This book is what contesters need
> To help their entries take the lead.

A quatrain consists of four lines which, in contest usage, may rhyme in three possible ways. In the most common version, only the second and fourth lines rhyme, thus:

> Within the pages of this book
> A lot of tips you'll find
> To make the entries that you write
> Become the winning kind.

In another form of quatrain, the second line rhymes with the first, while the fourth line rhymes with the third, thus:

> You needn't be so very wise
> To snare a handsome contest prize.
> You only need to take a look
> At winning lessons in this book.

In the third variation of this form, the first and third lines rhyme as do the second and fourth lines, thus:

> By learning how to handle rhyme,
> You'll set a winning pace.
> It may be used at any time
> To help you take first place.

THE LIMERICK

A limerick is a five-line verse in which the first, second, and fifth lines rhyme, and the third and fourth lines rhyme, thus:

> Many contests, perhaps, you have tried;
> But your entries were all cast aside.
> You can help yourself to win;
> Here's the way to begin—
> Learn the methods in Fell's Contest Guide!

All Are Jingles—Each Is Different

The same general theme has been deliberately used in all preceding examples to show you that similar ideas can easily be expressed in various forms of verse.

As previously noted, the term "jingle" is often applied indiscriminately to the couplets, quatrains, and limericks which are used in commercial contests.

While it is true that such two-line, four-line, and five-line rhymes are all jingles in a comprehensive sense, they must be considered separately in this book—for each type has a technique all its own, as will be demonstrated in following chapters dealing with these specific forms of verse.

Poetic Pointers

However, some fundamental facts about versification in general should be given now. These pointers apply to *all* rhymed stanzas, regardless of the number of lines they contain.

First, you should strive to use only *true rhymes*. For example, if you rhyme the word "date" with "mate," you would be quite correct; but if you tried to rhyme "date" with "made" you would be wrong.

Similar-sounding combinations like that are called *false rhymes* or *near rhymes*, and they should be avoided. While you may occasionally see such faults in published poems, that sort of error could cause your entry to be disqualified in a *contest*. Take care, therefore, to employ nothing but perfect rhymes.

Use a Rhyming Dictionary

Where, you may ask, may correct rhymes be found, if you can't think them up by yourself? The answer lies in a *rhyming* dictionary, which may be borrowed from any public library or purchased at any book store. (See Chapter 13, Sources of Success.)

To give yourself a fair chance at winning jingle contests, you should certainly possess your own copy of a good rhyming dictionary for ready reference—since you will be competing against experienced contesters who regularly use such assistance.

You've Got to Get Rhythm

In addition to proper rhyme, your versified entries should possess the right rhythm. This simply means that rhyming lines should match one another in accented words or syllables.

Some people recognize correct or incorrect rhythm almost instinctively. They seem to have an innate sense of swing, beat, or cadence. But whatever it may be called, this rhythmic recognition can be acquired by anyone through study of examples such as the following, in which words and syllables bearing a stronger stress or emphasis are capitalized to show where the accent naturally falls:

> NO one WINS by WISH-ing—
> FISH are CAUGHT by FISH-ing!

Note that this jingle has exactly the same number of syllables in each line—six. When reading it aloud (which is a good way to learn proper rhythm) you would normally place a heavier stress on the first, third, and fifth syllable of each line. You can plainly perceive, then, that the second line perfectly matches the cadence of the first line.

More Models to Follow

Of course, the number of words and syllables may vary greatly in different jingles—but, whether lines are short or long, their matching rhythm should be clearly apparent, as shown in these additional examples of varying lengths and styles utilized by most contest jingles:

Four syllables per line; accent on 2 and 4—

> All PRIZ-es GO
> to THOSE who KNOW.

Four syllables per line; accent on 1 and 3—

> LEARN by HEED-ing
> WHAT you're READ-ing.

Five syllables per line; accent on 2 and 5—

> This FAM-ous old BRAND
> Is FIRST in the LAND.

Six syllables per line; accent on 3 and 6—

> Once you've TEST-ed our TEA,
> It's the TOPS, you'll a-GREE.

Six syllables per line; accent on 2, 4 and 6—

> If YOU would LEAD the REST,
> You've GOT to DO your BEST.

Seven syllables per line; accent on 1, 3, 5 and 7—

> BOX tops, LA-bels, WRAP-pers, TOO,
> MAY be WORTH a LOT to YOU.

Eight syllables per line; accent on 2, 4, 6 and 8—

> It's FUN to PLAY the CON-test GAME,
> That LEADS, per-HAPS, to WEALTH and FAME.

Eight syllables per line; accent on 1, 3, 5 and 7—

> HERE's a CON-test WELL worth TRY-ing;
> GO and EN-ter . . . TIME is FLY-ing!

Nine syllables per line; accent on 3, 6 and 9—

> You can LEARN how to WIN by your WITS;
> Just keep TRY-ing and NEVer say "QUITS!"

In the chapters which follow, you will see how these varied patterns of rhyme and rhythm may be adapted to sing the praises of every product from absinthe to zweiback.

Chapter 4

HOW TO WIN COUPLET CONTESTS

Couplet contests fall into three categories:

1. Those requiring two complete rhyming lines entirely created by the entrant.

2. Those requiring the entrant to compose a second line rhyming with a single line given by the sponsor in the contest announcement.

3. Those requiring the entrant to finish the first line, containing only a starting phrase, and then to compose a second line rhyming with the first.

Several examples of each kind will be given for illustration.

Complete Couplets

Life Savers, one of America's most popular confections, once awarded prizes up to $500 each for two-line jingles describing various flavored candies. Following are typical winning entries:

> Butter Rum's a taste sensation—
> Sweetens "close-up" conversation.

> Two grand flavors, blended right;
> Butter Rum, a taste delight.

> Smooth, sweet Crysto-O-Mints are swell,
> As breath refreshers, they excel.

> For tangy flavor, breath protection,
> Wint-O-Green spells sweet perfection.

> Wint-O-Green, fresh and gay,
> Is my daily "Breath Bouquet."

> For after taste, a timely hint—
> Refresh yourself with Cryst-O-Mint.

The smoker's perfect "Go-Between"—
Minty, tangy Wint-O-Green.

For in-between, this smoker's hint—
Real old-fashioned Molas-O-Mint.

Adapt—and Win!

Note particularly the last three entries. The writer of the final example had read the two preceding winners when they were published earlier during the course of this weekly contest. Combining the rhyme of one with the idea of the other resulted in a winning entry for the observant contester.

This is a form of adaptation frequently encountered in successful entries. It proves the value to be derived from the study of winning entry examples, as given throughout this book, and especially in Chapter 15, Top Winning Entries, for your enlightenment and application. Chapter 13, Sources of Success, reveals additional sources of previous and current winners, so that you can keep abreast of this information—so vitally important to anyone aspiring to succeed in this highly competitive field.

Short and Sweet

Here are a few more complete couplets on a variety of products:

Bit-O-Honey is an energy quickie,
Always fresh and never sticky.

Every picture's a starry gem,
When it's labeled "M-G-M."

Mouth-watering flavor, wholesome blend,
Make Peter Paul my "confectionate" friend.

Pocket ease, drinking pleasure,
King Orange gives in double measure.

Flexible, washable, smooth and smart,
Crown Zippers star in every part.

Men agree, when beards are thickest,
Ingram's takes 'em off the quickest.

Crisco fills a housewife's need
For saving, satisfaction, speed.

Strong or weak—in this fine brew
The smooth rich flavor shines right through.

Fineline streamlines every letter,
Makes your writing look much better.

For delicious taste and no-spill protection,
Safe-T Cones are my first selection.

Add-a-Line Couplets

In these contests, the sponsor supplied one full line about some
product; and entrants were asked to add one rhyming line to complete the jingle.

Starting line: Almond Joy is a candy sensation . . .
Second lines:

> Best bar by far in my estimation.
> Nuts deluxe in delightful formation.
> Each sweet twin ought to win an ovation.
> Tops in taste-teasing candy temptation.

Starting line: I like Big Yank for eating right . . .
Second lines:

> For pep and punch it's "dine-a-mite."
> Adds nourishment to menus light.
> Recaptures pep that's taken flight.
> So fully packed with rich delight.
> Routs midday let-down for a mite.
> It won my love with my first bite.

Starting line: Albers Oats are best for me . . .
Second Lines:

> Restoring pep and energy.
> For outer glow and inner glee.
> An A-1 treat with Vitamin B.
> So much to like for little fee.

Follow the Leader

Some of these "second lines" may look quite simple; but they are not as easy to compose as they may seem. When you are given only a single starting line, instead of three or four lines as in other jingle contests, there is not much of a "plot" or theme to carry on. Yet you are expected to "follow the leader" as best you can.

In such cases, you must try to clothe the sponsor's bare beginning with the fanciest "word-robe" you can tailor to fit the given pattern. In the foregoing examples, most of the winners used such devices as alliteration, contrast, inner rhyme, paraphrase, and puns. Each of these winning tricks—and many more—will be fully explained and demonstrated in Chapter 6 on limericks.

Phrase-Finishing Couplets

Most popular among couplet contests are those presenting a starting phrase which the entrant must continue to form a first line and then add a second rhyming line to conclude the jingle. In this kind of contest, entrants have the advantage of choosing their own rhyming words, as shown in the varied examples which follow. In each stanza, the starting phrase given by the sponsor is separated by three dots (. . .) from the rest of the jingle composed by entrants.

While the products mentioned in these entries are well known and widely advertised, they will be briefly reviewed before each set of examples, so that you may clearly perceive how their particular virtues have been cleverly emphasized by successful contestants.

Soap-Praising Stanzas

Ads for Dial soap feature its protection against perspiration odor "around the clock." Described as pleasant to use, refreshing in effect, and good for one's complexion, Dial's *special quality* is said to be its deodorizing factor. Now see how winners have stressed this advertising point by relating specific benefits gained by using Dial soap.

> I'm glad I use Dial . . . I'm a social success,
> Since I learned how to bathe, as well as to dress.
>
> I'm glad I use Dial . . . it's so DIPlomatic;
> It flatters and soothes—leaves skin aromatic.

I'm glad I use Dial... my sales record confirms
It's the way to win friends and antagonize germs!

I'm glad I use Dial ... for romance never grows
When a feast for the eyes is a sock at the nose.

I'm glad I use Dial ... I use it exclusively,
Though it's hot where I labor, I sweat unobtrusively.

Lyrical Laundry Lines

Chiffon Flakes is another washing product of a different sort—
not for face or bath, but for laundry and kitchen usage. According
to its advertising, Chiffon is notable for its thorough yet gentle
cleansing power for fabrics and dishes—combining strength and
mildness to safeguard users' hands. Here's how some winning entrants brought out these advantages:

I like Chiffon ... for laundering perfection,
While giving hands such lotion-like protection.

I like Chiffon ... for *his* clothes and mine;
It's potent for heavy things and gentle for fine.

I like Chiffon ... such lamb-like suds
Get mulish dirt from all my duds.

I like Chiffon ... it's my wash friend true;
MENchanting blouses retain their hue.

I like Chiffon ... its sudsy swishes
Pamper my hands as they *prism* my dishes!

In the final example, note how the word "prism" has been used
with such original effect as a verb, alliterating with "pamper," to
suggest the sparkling brilliance of china and glassware when completely cleaned—by Chiffon Flakes, of course!

Read 'em and Reap!

You can now see that it pays to follow the contest sponsor's own
ads for his products. By using salient features from such ads as a
source of ideas for your jingles, you can be sure that the rhyme and
rhythm which you put into your lines will be based on sound reason
as well—and those are the three R's that will help you reap rich
rewards when trying entries in verse.

Chapter 5

HOW TO WIN QUATRAIN CONTESTS

Don't watch for the word "quatrain" to identify a contest calling for the addition of a fourth line to three given lines. "Quatrain" is used in this book to distinguish this particular form of verse from couplets and limericks. While that designation is definitely correct, you will not find it used by advertisers to describe contests of this kind, which they simply call "jingles."

However, you will have no trouble in recognizing quatrain contests, no matter what they're called. They all present three lines, to which you must add a rhyming fourth line to complete the verse.

Thousands of such contests have been held, and countless more are sure to come; but the few to be examined in this chapter typify their general structure and should serve to acquaint you with their winning requirements.

Million-Dollar Contest

Without question, the outstanding contest so far conducted in the four-line field was Lever Brothers' offer of one million dollars in prizes during 1961, promoting their full line of cleaning products.

Heralded as "the world's biggest contest," it offered more than 20,000 separate awards, topped by 27 Pontiac automobiles, for last lines to complete this jingle (which is repeated here without punctuation, exactly as it appeared on official entry blanks):

> A Million Dollar Contest and who could ask for more
> A Golden Opportunity is knocking at my door
> To try good Lever Products and be a winner too
> ....

According to the rules, the last word of the fourth line, to be composed by the entrant, had to rhyme with "too." This may seem too obvious for mention; but a large number of inexperienced contesters, in such a case as this, would surely have attempted to compose lines rhyming with "door" unless clearly directed to the proper word to be rhymed.

Standards for Success

The judging standards and system of rating entries for this contest were clearly stated in the rules. Since many current jingle contests have similar criteria, you should carefully consider this excerpt from the Lever Brothers rules, which served as the basis for selection of winners:

APPROPRIATENESS (appropriate to follow the lead lines, and
    appropriate as to rhyme and meter): Up to 35 points.
FRESHNESS (interest, creativeness, sparkle): Up to 25 points.
CLARITY (suitable and effective use of words): Up to 25 points.
SINCERITY (believability): Up to 15 points.

To understand the significance of these rating standards, you must see how well they apply to a random dozen winning lines which are typical of those that proved successful in this contest.

Victors on View

New shine to hopes—new pride in home—these bonus brands imbue.

With "help" adept and hope aglow, I'm doubly well-to-do.

I cannot lose, for when I use this brand rewards ensue.

Here's one more first by Lever that again none can outdo.

With Lever aids, I've leisure time to bag a bonus coup.

I'd travel into "Easy Street" through "Lever Avenue"!

With Lever to look out for me, my outlook's bright in hue.

Saves time and cents, enriches home while prizes I pursue.

No second knock required—this chance I won't eschew!

With "Lever" on the label, results to prize ensue.

My gift, a lift in household chores—no task they can't subdue.

Awards this wife much richer life—less grime, more time, prize coup!

Why They Won

Examine these lines thoroughly. Observe exactly *what* they say and *how* they say it. Note that each last word rhymes perfectly with "too." Read the lines aloud in singsong style to grasp their cadence or meter, matching the rhythm of the third line.

Then you'll notice in what manner each winning entry, in its own particular way, possesses the qualities sought by the judges of this contest—appropriateness, freshness, clarity, and sincerity. These essential features were achieved by the winners through their skillful use of such different methods as alliteration, repetition, contrast, inner rhyme, word play, figures of speech, balanced phrases, unique approach, personalized reaction, or unusual rhyming word.

Why They Lost

To understand even better why these entries won, consider a couple of Lever lines that failed to make the grade. Here's one:

What better way to "clean up" could anyone pursue?

This line has proper rhythm and correct rhyme, and also a play on the term "clean up" with its double meaning of "washing" and "winning money." At first glance, it may seem fairly clever and quite appropriate. But thousands of similar—if not identical—lines must have been submitted, since the "clean-up" idea was so obvious for the Lever contest subject.

Therefore, all such entries completely lacked one of the major winning qualifications—*freshness*—and consequently were discarded because of duplication.

Another non-winner was:

For LEVER can work wonders—as Archimedes knew!

This is certainly an original line, which hardly could have been duplicated by any other entrant. It also makes some sense—*provided* the reader knows that the ancient Greek physicist, Archimedes, discovered the principle of a lever's power. But the allusion was much too erudite and far-fetched for use in this contest; and the entry was thrown out for lack of clarity and appropriateness.

You can see, then, how important it is to make your own entries rate high in the specific qualities which the rules request. Additional ways to do so are illustrated in the following examples from other quatrain contests.

Matching Meter

> Good grooming aids are now a must
> And COLGATE is the name to trust
> For sparkling teeth and skin and hair
> ....

The outstanding feature of this unfinished jingle is its perfection of meter. Not all commercial verse contests offer jingles that are so absolutely correct in rhythm. Note that all words in each line are naturally accented in exactly the same way: da-DUM, da-DUM, da-DUM, da-DUM. That is, the stress or heavier beat falls on syllables 2-4-6-8 of every line, including the one to be rhymed:

> For SPARK-ling TEETH and SKIN and HAIR

When a contest jingle is so carefully contrived, you may be sure that one of the first things the judges will look for (after correct rhyme, of course!) is proper rhythm, to match the meter of the given stanza. You will find this quality in every one of the winning lines presented here.

More Winning Ways

As you probably realize by now, it takes more than perfect rhyme and rhythm to achieve success in last-line contests—and each of these examples has that *extra factor* which made it a winner, as indicated by classification:

ALLITERATION

I'm spick and span, no speck they spare.

Make sense, save cents, with scents so rare.

ANALOGY
(see Chapter 12, Analogy in Action)

That make Eyes DANCE, win Head A STARE.

Use "Colgate Street" to reach "Charm Square."

COINED WORD

"Groomerrily" with Colgate's flair.

Unveils "glowtential" hidden there.

CONTRAST

Are prized from crib to easy chair.

Will give Plain Jane a glamour air.

DOUBLE MEANING

"It's WIFE-WINSURANCE!" men declare.

These handle "U.S. Male" with care.

INNER RHYME

Such CARE helps SNARE a solitaire.

With CARE so FAIR none can compare.

Literary Lines

Finest examples of non-commercial winners are these, from a contest conducted by Sears in Milwaukee, which offered a Chevrolet car as first prize for finishing this verse:

> Wisconsin Autumn scenes today
> Await you in Sears' Chevrolet;
> The lakes and glens and farmlands neat
> ....

Each winning line employed a recognizable contest device, though phrased in polished literary style:

Rest russet robed in God's retreat. (*alliteration*)

Sing Earthly Anthems Richly Sweet. (*acrostic—the initial letters spell "SEARS"*)

Are nature's roto-color sheet. (*analogy*)

Are ample cause for "Wisconceit"! (*coined word*)

Unfold, enthrall, inspire, entreat. (*emphasis*)

Making the Most of the Least

In the Lever contest, entrants could employ as many as fourteen syllables for their last lines. In the Sears and Colgate contests, only eight syllables were available. What can one do when no more than six syllables may be used? Plenty—as these examples from the Alcoa Wrap contest will show:

> Super-strength Alcoa Wrap,
> The strongest you can buy,
> Is helpful in so many ways
> . . . .

Unlike the other contests cited in this chapter, which required entries to rhyme with the third line, endings for this jingle were supposed to rhyme with its *second* line, accented on syllable 2-4-6, thus:

> The STRONG-est YOU can BUY

In these winning lines, note how various techniques have been used to make them different and outstanding:

> Foil toil—Alcoa-fy! (inner rhyme; coined word)
>
> Foods "cap and gown" supply. (analogy)
>
> Yule trims 'twill GLOW-rify. (coined word)
>
> For ripless wrap—drip dry. (alliteration; inner rhyme)
>
> For "big cheese" or "small fry." (contrast; humor)
>
> Bids taste-leak, waste-pique—bye! (double inner rhyme)

There's a lesson to learn from that final Alcoa example, which was reported to be a major prize winner. Its last word, "bye," is not an actual rhyme for "buy" in the second line, since the two words are pronounced exactly alike. Real rhymes start with different letters, ending with the same sound.

However, in this particular case, the exceptionally clever pair of rhyming words *within* the line—"taste-leak, waste-pique"—apparently carried it to victory despite identical usage of the "buy" sound. Hence, in similar jingle contests, you may consider it permissible to do likewise—but only when the *rest* of your line is good enough to compensate for repetition of the same rhyme sound in your last word.

To sum up, you can see that the number of words or syllables available for your last line is not so important. It's how you use them that counts—and the fewer allowed, the greater the challenge to your ingenuity!

Chapter 6

HOW TO WIN LIMERICK CONTESTS

Of all rhyming competitions, limerick contests are undoubtedly the most popular. As far back as 1908, a British newspaper awarded a huge prize for the line finishing this limerick:

> There was a young lady of Ryde
> Whose locks were consid'rably dyed
>   The hue of her hair
>   Made everyone stare ...
>
> *"She's piebald, she'll die bald," they cried.*

Almost three-quarters of a century later, contests based on limericks are going stronger than ever before in their hilarious history. However, during that time, limericks have undergone a marked change in content, though not in form.

For Fun and Funds

The humorous limerick contest, calling for an amusing last line, still appears occasionally in magazines or newspapers, either for the entertainment of readers or as a circulation builder. But by far the widest usage of limericks is now made in commercial contests, to promote the sale of various products. They are also used in campaigns for many worthy causes, such as safe driving, fire prevention, and charitable fund raising. Product-praising limericks generally pay the highest prizes of all.

There is, of course, a considerable difference between limericks created solely for laughs and those that convey a sales or campaign message. Both versions will be given appropriate attention here.

Because of the widespread popularity of limerick contests—which greatly outnumber those based on couplets or quatrains—this chapter contains more comprehensive instructions for composing limerick last lines than were accorded the other two types. Bear in mind, though, that every winning technique described for limericks can be applied with equal success to couplet and quatrain contests, as well as to most other commercial or even literary competitions in which light verse plays a part.

What Makes a Limerick

When starting to work on a limerick contest—whether commercial or not—you should make a careful study of the four lines given by the sponsor. Repeat them aloud (as with *all* jingles) to note which syllables are accented. Grasping the rhythm of the first two lines is most important, since your own fifth line should have the same beat or swing as lines 1 and 2, as well as rhyming with them.

In nearly every limerick you encounter, you will find only two variations in the rhythmic pattern of its first two lines. One style places the heaviest accent on syllables 3-6-9:

> Here's an ICE cream you'll EAT with de-LIGHT,
> Starting NOW, when the SEAS-on is RIGHT.

In the other model, the stress falls on syllables 2-5-8:

> "I WON-der who's MILK-ing her NOW,"
> Said REU-ben, who FARMED out his COW.

The same sequence of heavier accents will also be found in limericks whose lines end with extra unstressed syllables, as shown:

> Here's a QUES-tion that PUZZ-les a BUY-er—(3-6-9)
> Will my CUR-rent bills CLIMB ever HIGH-er? (3-6-9)

> A DEAL-er in OR-anges STA-ted (2-5-8)
> "With SUN-kist I'm AL-ways e-LA-ted." (2-5-8)

Although your fifth line should preferably match the meter of the first two lines, as previously mentioned, it is permissible to mix 2-5-8 and 3-6-9 patterns, since they sound so much alike. In fact, *both* rhythmic beats appear in the starting lines of many limericks, like this:

> A KITCH-en is NO place to STAY (2-5-8)
> On a WON-derful SUN-shiny DAY (3-6-9)

In such cases, your own line may follow *either* pattern.

48

Aside from the purely mechanical requirement of proper rhyme and rhythm your line must possess some distinctive feature to give it a good chance of winning. To achieve this outstanding quality, you should employ one or more of the following methods, which have proved successful in countless limerick contests.

1. ALLITERATION—using two or more words starting with the same letters:

> Here's a grand way to start the day right;
> Serve prunes to your family's delight.
>> With milk or with cream
>> They are simply supreme . . .
>
> To BRing you a BReakfast that's BRight!

> There was a young husband named Bill
> Who never could quite get his fill.
>> Cold cuts he'd demand—
>> Swift's Premium Brand . . .
>
> Finding Favor in Flavors That Thrill!

> "Can I handle a car!" Alec crowed,
> As he sneered at a slippery road.
>> You can guess what he did—
>> He went into a skid . . .
>
> Now Alec is Sad, Sued, and Sewed.

> Now's the time for some brisk Lipton Tea.
> It's the Change of Pace drink, you'll agree.
>> You've gulped coffee all day,
>> So you're ready to say . . .
>
> "It's Pekoe for Perk-up Piquancy!"

2. ANALOGY—adapting appropriate words from some entirely different field or subject:

> Coke in family-size is ideal
> To serve at a party or meal;
>> So get a supply
>> Of each size when you buy . . .
>
> Be an ACE with FULL HOUSE on this DEAL

> Having tried Kayser's new "Nimble-Nee,"
> I'm convinced it's the best hose for me.
>> With comfort and beauty,
>> It does double duty . . .
>
> SCORES a HIT without RUNS, I can see!

> If you cannot see much very far,
> You shouldn't be driving a car.
>> It's all for the best
>> To have an eye test . . .
>
> Sight PRESERVED, in a JAM saves a JAR!

> There's no other coffee today
> As good as the new Nescafe.
>> Its flavor beats ground,
>> Saves money per pound . . .
>
> It's TAILORED to SUIT each gourmet.

Chapter 12, "Analogy in Action," cites many winning examples, and further explains analogies.

3. COINED WORDS—creating a unique word or expression by combining, dividing, or altering ordinary words:

> Of course, we all need relaxation,
> But let's make it safe recreation.
>> For a mishap—just one!—
>> Could spoil all your fun . . .
>
> VACAUTION's the need of our nation!

A lady in search of romance
Embarked on a liner for France.
"I do hope," said she
"To marry at sea ...

"Which accounts for my NAUGHTY-GAL glance."

For fresh, home-cooked soups that are best,
Lipton Soup Mixes outdo the rest.
A cinch to prepare—
Taste beyond all compare ...

It's SOUPERB—for convenience compressed.

4. COLORATION—using color words literally or figuratively, preferably with colored ink or crayon for indicated shade:

If grass cutting is getting you down,
And lawn care is making you frown,
You need more than a toy,
Buy yourself a Lawn Boy ...

Keep your GREEN in the PINK 'stead of BROWN!

A smart little lady named Kay
Looks for Phillips 66 on her way.
The stations are clean
The service is keen ...

Car in PINK spares "long GREEN" and BLUE day!

A youngster once got on the sly
Explosives for Fourth of July.
When his father found out
What the kid was about ...

He saw RED, then turned WHITE, and BLEW high!

5. COMPARISON—using picturesque, striking, or unusual terms in descriptive relation to the subject:

Away the blithe pennies will roll
When cold isn't under control;
   But, give Leonard a trial,
   Its bright Master Dial . . .

Guards expense like a Scot on the dole.

There's no point in wasting your dough
On a freezer that freezes too slow.
   For freezing that's faster
   The Leonard's the master . . .

For it's cold as a North Polar floe.

6. CONTRAST—using antonyms or words of opposite meaning:

"These soap flakes are sure a delight,"
Said a clever young housewife named Wright.
   "In my washing machine
   They get clothes so clean . . .

"OLD or NEW, LOTS or FEW, come out bright."

You're a careful, sharp driver, you say?
You can use this advice anyway:
   You need not be scared,
   But be always prepared . . .

To protect your TOMORROWS TODAY!

A pretty young housewife named Poe
Found dishwashing dreary and slow;
   Till she tried Oxydol—
   Speed soap of them all . . .

(a) Just right—suds HIGH and cost LOW!

(b) Saw suds GREAT from a LITTLE soap grow.

(c) Now her WORK is like PLAY, we all know.

7. DOUBLE MEANINGS—using words which have a secondary connotation:

To college Dad sent his son, Jack,
Paying bills every year by the stack.
  Now what can Dad show
  For spending that dough?

All he got was a lone QUARTER BACK!

There is a young fellow named Spence
Who knows what to do with five cents.
  Kraft candy he brings
  To his girl friend who sings:

"Such FRESHNESS NO BUDDY resents!"

Once you sleep on a Sealy, you'll say:
"What a mattress! It's strictly okay!"

  Neither too soft nor hard,
  With its new Comfort-Gard . . .

For the REST OF YOUR LIFE, sleep this way.

There is a new wrestler in town,
Who knows just the right time to frown.
  He grunts and he groans,
  He bites and he moans . . .

Case of WHINES and SHAM PAIN for this clown.

8. HOMONYMS—using two words in the same line that sound or look alike, but have different meanings:

All your cleaning is easy as pie
When Old Dutch is the cleanser you buy.
  It's new and it's quicker
  And safer and slicker . . .

(a) For small CHANGE, a big CHANGE in one try.

(b) Cleans all WARE with no WEAR, scent or sigh.

(c) For the SPRING in SPRING Cleaning, just try!

Calvin Keene thought the road was his own,
That his seat at the wheel was a throne.
    But his kingdom has crumbled,
    King Cal is now humbled . . .

"How I've RUED being RUDE!" hear him moan.

Mary's cakes filled her heart with distress,
Some were good—some were simply a mess.
    Then the Softasilk way
    She discovered one day . . .

"It's the FLOWER of FLOURS," she'll confess.

9. INNER RHYME—words that rhyme within your line, other than the last word:

"Evervess," cried a husband named Pete,
"Is a mixer than cannot be beat.
    "You save half a dime
    "On a bottle each time . . .

"There's more BOUNCE in each OUNCE—what a treat!"

Safe Oxydol washes clothes white;
Mild Camay helps keep your skin right.
    Don't take it from me—
    Use both and you'll see . . .

Suds proFUSE make their USE a delight.

Marie had a lot of ambition
For movie and stage recognition.
    But the nearest she got
    Was the hat-checking spot . . .

For she SPURNED every DURNED proposition.

A lovely young lady named Mode,
Whose sport car would burn up the road,
    Tried to make it step more
    With her foot on the floor ...

(a) When a TURN made an URN her abode.

(b) End of SCRIPT: In a CRYPT Mode is stowed.

10. PARODY or PARAPHRASE—changing a well-known
expression to fit a new subject:

There once was a motorist gay;
He was—but he isn't today!
    He got by for a while
    But he drove his last mile ...

(a) "When the BREW of the night" blurred the way.

(b) He "went down with his SIP" so they say.

(c) He learned "a BAD TURN" doesn't pay.

American Buslines are new,
Giving fast, friendly service to you.
    Our bus fares are low,
    Wherever you go ...

Spare the "High Cost of LEAVING" all through.

The new Simoniz method is slick,
Gives you six months' protection—but quick!
    Liquid Kleener's the clue
    That cuts work-time for you ...

Putting "Age BEHIND Beauty"—slick trick!

11. PERSONIFICATION—attributing human or living characteristics to inanimate objects or abstract ideas:

"Delicious!" said John to his mate,
"It's the best soup that I ever ate!"
   "It's Lipton's, my honey,
   "And saving you money." . . .

(a) Working gal's pantry PAL CANDIDATE.

(b) Garden tang SPRINGS TO LIFE in your plate.

Lend a hand in the safety crusade—
In public, at home, at your trade.
   The lift that you give
   Will help other folks live . . .

You'll find Courtesy LEADS THE PARADE!

12. PUNS—altering the sound, spelling or meaning of words for humorous effect:

There once was a dude from Hoboken
Whose pony had not yet been broken.
   He got on his saddle
   And sat down a-straddle . . .

But he got the BRONC'S CHEER—quite outspoken!

A charming homemaker named Lou
Kept her home very tidy, it's true.
   But her pride took a fall
   On a rug in the hall . . .

Don't let FALL-TY housekeeping trip you!

There was a young fellow named Ferd,
Who thought he could fly like a bird.
   He built wings, the poor stiff,
   And jumped off a cliff . . .

'Twasn't (W)RIGHT—only ORVILLE absurd.

13. REPETITION—repeating the same or similar words, phrases or sounds:

> A much courted lady named May
> Served Rath's Black Hawk Ham every day.
>   "If a girl wants a man, sir,"
>   Said she, "Here's the answer . . .
>
> "No MISS MISSES MRS. my way!"
>
> The new Simoniz method's a breeze,
> Gives six months' protection with ease.
>   Liquid Kleener cuts grime
>   So it save half your time . . .
>
> Lets VINTAGE cars VANTAGE looks seize.
>
> This swivel-top cleaner's for me,
> I get "reach-easy" cleaning, you see.
>   Cleaning ceiling-to-floor
>   Isn't hard any more . . .
>
> This GOOD BUY bids "GOOD-BYE, Drudgery!"

14. TRIADS—expressing three different sales points or ideas in a trio of phrases, often combined with Inner Rhyme:

> Yes, Esquire Boot Polish is best,
> It will pass every shoe shining test,
>   Lanolizes your shoes,
>   It's the polish to use . . .

(a) Style's retained, shoes are stained, cleaned and dressed.

(b) Steps up glow, slows bruise woe, tops the rest.

(c) Rebuffs nick, reshines quick, retints best.

57

The minerals that help you feel swell
And vitamins that help keep you well
   Are in prunes that you serve
   In dishes with verve . . .

Good in taste, good in looks, good in smell.

15. TRIPLE RHYME—similar to Inner Rhyme, but using words
within the line that also rhyme with its last word:

   It's delicious, it's smooth, it's a treat;
   For dessert, Frostee cannot be beat.
      It's so easy to make,
      Gives your budget a break . . .

   You'll DEFEAT summer HEAT with this SWEET!

   "Just one of those things," muttered Lew.
   "It happened to me, 'stead of you."
      But Lew shouldn't have yelped,
      For it could have been helped . . .

   Had LEW asked a FEW what they KNEW.

16. TYPOGRAPHICAL TRICKS—using initials, abbreviations,
or unusual effects, such as upside-down lines:

   When Elsie went out for a spin,
   Her car made a deafening din.
      So she lifted the hood
      And at once understood . . .

   ¡uᴉɥʇᴉʍ ǝɹǝʍ sʞɹoʍ ǝɥʇ ʍoɥ s,ǝɹǝɥ ɹoℲ

   "I'm terr-r-ribly fond of good tea,"
   Said Sandy MacTavish MacFee.
      "It must have fine flavor
      To meet with my favor . . .

   "So U C Y I U's A & P."

Driver Dan let his busy mind stray
From the wheel to a home chore that day;
    Then discovered too late
    That he must concentrate ...

Absent mind made him wind up this way!

To be at your sparkling best,
Drink Coke for its pleasure and zest.
    Refreshing and bright,
    Its flavor's just right ...

*C*heerful *O*ffering *K*eenly *E*xpressed!

The final example is an Acrostic, in which the first letters of the four words in the last line spell the product's name, COKE. This is a difficult trick to manage in a single limerick line; but when well done is almost certain to win a prize. See the Sears jingle winner in Chapter 5 for another excellent example of this technique.

Testing Your Own Lines

Before submitting any last line to a limerick contest, analyze it yourself to see whether it possesses most—if not all—of these features, which are always desirable and sometimes essential:

Is your line correct in rhyme and rhythm?

Is it appropriate to the subject?

Is it clearly worded and easily understandable?

Does it praise some particular virtues of the product (in a commercial contest)?

Does it contain a different, unique idea—rather than the obvious one?

Does it conclude the story or message in the given lines in a smooth, natural, and logical manner?

Does it contain one or more of the success secrets revealed in this chapter?

What the Sponsor Wants

As a final commentary on limericks, Harry S. Granatt once wrote wittily in the Portland *Oregon Journal*:

A limerick packs laughs anatomical
Into space that is quite economical.
　　But the good ones I've seen
　　So seldom are clean—
And the clean ones so seldom are comical!

While that may be true of many popular limericks, all quoted here are quite clean and some are fairly funny, too. But it must be remembered that *humor is not sought in most commercial contests*. What such sponsors want are sales points and product benefits. You've seen how to *convey* those ideas in various ways. Where to *find* them is another matter, which will be taken up in following chapters.

Chapter 7

HOW TO WIN STATEMENT CONTESTS—IN PROSE

If limericks are the most popular form of rhyming contests, then surely statements are the most popular of *all* contests. The reason for this is easy to understand. Many people have no knack for writing in rhyme. While that art can be learned—as demonstrated in preceding chapters—it takes some effort to acquire skill with verse. But prose is the natural expression of everyone who can write at all.

Therefore, contests calling for prose statements have a universal appeal. An ad may proclaim: "Win a fortune! Just tell why you like Baker's Bread in 25 words or less." Reading that announcement, the average person will immediately think: "That sounds easy. I guess I'll try it."

In the United States, a nationally advertised statement contest offering ample awards will often draw millions of entries. Vast numbers of people are attracted to such an offer—not only by its huge prizes, but because that kind of contest seems so simple and easy to enter.

However, despite their popularity, statement contests are not as easy to win as they may appear—as myriads of hopeful entrants eventually discover to their disappointment.

To compose successful statements, you must first understand *exactly* what this sort of contest requires, then learn the methods of filling those requirements in ways that will please the judges who select the winners.

Read the Rules Carefully

In most statement contests, the first rule will read something like this: "Complete this statement in 25 words or less: *I like Brand Name Product because . . .*" That means you must use only *one* sentence to finish the starting phrase. You may break it up with commas, dashes, semi-colons, or other punctuation—but don't use a period until the very end of your single sentence.

Know the Product

Before you even start to write a statement for any commercial contest, you should become thoroughly familiar with the product involved. If it is an inexpensive item, buy it, use it, observe its qualities. If the subject is something costly, like a car, refrigerator, or television set, visit a dealer for descriptive literature. Study all the ads you can find about the product—and file them for future reference. Notice what features are stressed in the manufacturer's own advertising.

After learning as much as you can about the contest product, from ads and from personal use when possible, your next step is to compile a list of appropriate words and phrases to describe the product and your reactions to it. For example, if you intend to compose entries about a breakfast food, your list might include such expressions as these:

appetizing	health-building	thrifty
delicious	inviting	vitalizing
energy-rich	nourishing	wholesome
full-flavored	savory	zestful

Some of these words you can think up yourself. Some you can borrow from the product's ads. Others you'll find in your dictionary or thesaurus by seeking synonyms or related terms.

While such word-lists are essential in preparing to compose statements (as well as other kinds of entries), they provide only the bricks with which you will build a complete structure. You still need detailed plans to guide you in developing your material from basic idea to finished form.

Twenty Techniques for Triumph

In the following models, you will see how well-chosen words are put together in different designs to achieve winning effects. Included here is every major technique available for the successful creation of statements "in 25 words or less."

Since most of these methods were defined in the preceding chapter on limericks, their meaning need not always be given; but the examples will clearly demonstrate their use. In all cases, the sponsor's own starting phrase is separated from the entry proper by three dots (...), and words or letters of special significance are capitalized.

1. ACROSTICS

In this device, words are selected and arranged to convey an appropriate message while spelling out vertically the name of the product or sponsor with the initial letters of each line, as shown:

I read *Movie Guide* because . . .

> *M* ovie Guide,
> *O* ffering
> *V* aried and
> *I* nteresting
> *E* ntertainment,
>
> *G* ives
> *U* s all the
> *I* nformation we
> *D* esire for full
> *E* njoyment of film fare.

In a double acrostic, which is more difficult to construct, a *second* vertical word appears within the lines, as in this example:

I like Sunkist Oranges best because . . .

S	uperior to all	*O*	thers,
U	nequalled for	*R*	ichness,
N	utritious and	*A*	ppetizing,
K	nown for extra	*N*	ectar
I	n every golden	*G*	lobe,
S	unkist oranges	*E*	xcel
T	hroughout in	*S*	atisfaction.

2. ALLITERATION

I want to see New York's World's Fair because . . . as a Native New Yorker, I know that this Exciting, Exhilarating Exposition will Make Me More Mindful of our Marvelous Metropolis!

The Pepsi-Cola home carton is our family's favorite because . . . we know our P's and Q's—Plenty Quantity of Purest Quality makes the Perfect Quencher for Pleasing Quickly.

I changed to Chase and Sanborn's Coffee because . . . choicest coffees for Flavor, expert blending for Fragrance, dating for Freshness make it Delicious to Drink, Delightful to smell, Dependable to buy.

3. ANALOGY

Atomic theme:

I like Albers Oatmeal because . . . it's the NUCLEUS of a solid breakfast, with food ELEMENTS skillfully COMPOUNDED for maximum ENERGY—a POWERFUL WEAPON against undernourishment.

Card theme:

I would like to spend a vacation at the Deauville Hotel in Miami Beach because . . . STAYING at this KING of Gold Coast hotels, I'd find a great DEAL of ROYAL entertainment, to leave me FLUSH FULL of fun!

Political theme:

I serve my guests Pepsi-Cola because . . . it's my CANDIDATE for the FAVORITE American drink, its PLATFORM is delicious flavor plus economy, and it WINS VOTES at all PARTIES.

For more on *analogy*, see Chapter 12.

4. BALANCED BENEFITS

This technique, not previously explained, consists of paired words and phrases—with each pair citing *two* equally important product virtues that benefit the user.

I like Calox because . . . it BRIGHTENS my teeth WITHOUT BUFFING away their precious enamel—the only dentifrice that combines such SAFETY in action with such EFFECTIVENESS in results.

I like Styl-Eez Shoes best because . . . being SURE-FIT-TED, they make me SURE-FOOTED—with COMFORT that puts PEP in my STEP, and STYLE that puts PRIDE in my STRIDE!

5. COINED WORDS

Years ago, the best place to observe current word coinage in action was in Walter Winchell's column, where one could find freshly minted Winchellisms almost every day. Examples from his famous newspaper feature will appear in a later chapter on Naming Contests; but here is how a clever entrant artfully used several original coined words in a winning statement:

Insist on Champion Spark Plugs because ... TREK-SPERTS know Champion's exclusive construction plugs moisture and MUCKUMULATIONS that reduce POW-ERFORMANCE, sparks instant ignition, nimble EXCE-LERATION—triggering unsurpassed durability and PURRABILITY.

As you may perceive, these unusual creations were achieved by combining ordinary words, such as trek experts (treksperts); muck accumulations (muckumulations); power performance (Powerformance); excelling acceleration (exceleration); and purring—meaning smooth-running—ability (purrability).

6. COLORATION

This device is best adapted for subjects which lend themselves naturally to it; but may also be used for general contest topics.

I use Tintex dyes because . . . when my budget is in the RED and faded dresses make me BLUE, Tintex puts them in the PINK and makes life COLORFUL again!

I use Super Suds because ... it WHITENS without BLUING, never REDDENS my hands, and saves "long GREEN" by keeping sheets from YELLOWING with age.

I like Wheaties because . . . these GOLDEN flakes turn BLUE mornings into ROSY dawns, keep my family's health in the PINK and our food budget out of the RED.

I don't drink liquor because . . . alcohol may cause a RED nose, a WHITE liver, a YELLOW streak, a DARK BROWN breath, and a BLUE outlook.

7. COMPARISON

I like Albers Corn Flakes because . . . they are crisp as a winter morning, fresh as a spring shower, and inviting as a summer breeze—the perfect year-round breakfast food.

I use Camay Soap because . . . I've found Camay as gentle as cold cream, as soothing as a lotion, and as fragrant as party perfume.

I enjoy driving a Chevrolet because . . . it starts like a shot, runs like a rabbit, handles like a polo pony, climbs like a mountain goat, and stops like a pillowed fist.

8. CONTRAST

I want to see Seattle's Century 21 Exposition because . . . born in the long-gone PAST, I want to be PRESENT at the FUTURE to learn TODAY how life will look in that distant TOMORROW.

I like Shurfine Coffee because . . . every cup is "TOPS" clear down to the BOTTOM.

Lighters appeal to me more than matches because . . . lighters are graceful, matches are awkward; lighters are modern, matches are old-fashioned; lighters are safe, matches are ·dangerous; lighters are clean, matches are messy.

I prefer Nectar Tea because . . . many years of expert blending form the BACKGROUND which places flavor-fresh Nectar Tea in the FOREGROUND as my favorite.

9. DOUBLE MEANINGS

I prefer Sunkist oranges because . . . I can STRAIN quantities of rich, vitamin-packed juice from this naturally ripened fruit with no STRAIN on our food budget.

The Pepsi-Cola Home Carton is our family's favorite because . . . we get a "BREAK" in its extra content, but never a BREAK in its extra storing container.

10. HUMAN INTEREST

Entries in this category derive greater effect from the writer's personal status, condition, or circumstances than they do from clever wording.

I keep Oxydol on hand because . . . my husband, an iron worker, gets his clothes extra dirty—but I can always depend on Oxydol to clean them quicker with less effort.

I like Spry best for all baking and frying because . . . as a cook, I appreciate its easy blending—as a mother, its freshness and wholesomeness—as a housewife, its much-needed economy.

I like Camay because . . . though radium therapy cured my skin trouble, it left my skin real tender; but Camay's soft, kind lather always feels refreshing and soothing to it.

11. MATCHING WORDS

This device employs several words with the same suffix or rhyming sound, strategically placed to link various phrases for unified effect.

The features I like best about Palm Beach suits are . . . their ADAPTABILITY for all occasions, DURABILITY despite lightness, WASHABILITY if soiled—adding up to all-round SUITABILITY.

I like to trade at Crown Drug Stores because . . . courtesy GREETS me when I enter, economy MEETS me when I buy, and satisfaction TREATS me when I use their products.

I like Pique Kitchen Magic because . . . it AMPLIFIES natural food flavors, GLORIFIES commonplace dishes, INTENSIFIES taste appeal of vegetables, MINIFIES expense of good meals, and GRATIFIES every appetite.

I like new super-speed Old Dutch Cleanser because . . . it DEFEATS grease, grime and hard water scum, DELETES scratching, scraping and time-taking toil, and BEATS every cleansing aid in ease, effectiveness and economy.

12. PARAPHRASE OR PARODY

These entries are modelled after well-known expressions, or they include popular sayings, suitably altered to fit the subject.

I joined the March of Dimes because . . . you can do so much, for so many, for so little.

This car-winning entry is evidently a paraphrase of the latter part of Winston Churchill's classic tribute to the Royal Air Force: "Never in the field of human conflict was *so much owed by so many to so few*." Incidentally, the name "March of Dimes" itself is derived from another famous title, "The March of Time."

Parker pens make fine gifts because . . . they are First in Worth, First in Style, and First in the Choice of Recipients.

This is obviously based on the Washington eulogy: "First in war, first in peace, and first in the hearts of his countrymen."

I switched to Salem Cigarettes because . . . after trying many other brands, I found LOVE AT FIRST LIGHT in Salem's refreshingly different taste that makes a smoke TOO GOOD TO BE THROUGH.

In this example, you can readily recognize parodies on two popular phrases: "love at first sight" and "too good to be true."

13. PERSONIFICATION

The first entry that follows (which won $5,000 for its composer) is an exceptionally fine example of *personification*—in this case, attributing human features and feelings to a floor mop. The second entry (also a major prize winner) employs the same technique to humanize the writer's budget and thus emphasize one of the coffee product's benefits—its low price.

My favorite O-Cedar product is O-Cedar Floor Mop because . . . its NOSE pokes efficiently into corners; its

NECK bends OBLIGINGLY under furniture; its O-Ce-darized FINGERS quickly gather dust and "witches-wool," leaving floors immaculate, shining.

I like Shurfine Coffee because . . . there is a bonus of fine flavor in every cup and its price makes my budget SIT UP AND SMILE!

14. PROBLEMS

Like "human interest" entries, problem statements gain their greatest effect from the difficulty described and its solution by the product, without relying much on method of presentation.

I like Ivory Soap because . . . though I live in a soft-coal town, Ivory enables me to keep my organdy curtains and bedspreads as fresh and clean as new.

I keep Dreft on hand because . . . with two families using one kitchen, getting through quicker is necessary; and Dreft helps because it always gets my dishes thoroughly cleaned in less time.

15. PUNS

Generally used for humorous effect, this device may be employed in commercial contests where a light touch does not seem amiss.

I prefer coffee freshly roasted by my grocer because . . . I'd rather have my coffee properly roasted before I use it than to have it "roasted" by my guests after drinking it.

I like those tiny little tea leaves in Tetley because . . . these sunburst-of-flavor leaves give consist-ently satisfying, lip-smacking goodness—with more PERK-UP PER CUP and less "WAIST" per sip.

16. RELATED TERMS

In this technique, you wield several related words to weld your entry together.

I like Sunsweet Prunes because . . . they are vitamin-rich—GOOD for my family; tenderized for quick-cook-ing—BETTER for me; and inexpensive—BEST for my pocketbook.

The new Rambler appeals to me because . . . it is HIGH in power and mileage; WIDE for comfort and convenience; and as HANDSOME in performance as appearance.

I like to shop at Rexall stores because . . . outstanding service wins my APPLAUSE, competent prescription clerks win my APPROVAL, bargain values in nationally advertised merchandise win my APPRECIATION.

I use Dr. Lyon's Tooth Powder because . . . BEHIND it are many years of reliable manufacture; IN it, proven cleansing ingredients in economical powder form; AFTER it, sweet breath and a sparkling smile.

17. REPETITION

I prefer Sheffield Milk because . . . coming from the finest farms, it LEADS IN SELECTION; given ultramodern processing, it LEADS IN PERFECTION; delivered with extra care, it LEADS IN PROTECTION.

Ground Gripper Shoes are the most comfortable because . . . they STAND OUT for perfect fit; STAND UP during long wear; STAND OFF discomfort; STAND BY with arch support; and are delightful to STAND IN.

18. REVERSAL

This rather difficult but effective device consists of *transposing words* in one phrase to get a reversed result in the following phrase.

I like Kellogg's Special K Cereal because . . . while low in calorie content, it's packed with vitamins and minerals that will add YEARS TO MY LIFE and LIFE TO MY YEARS.

I think it's wise to wear Safety Shoes because . . . their positive protection helps to KEEP ME ON MY TOES and to KEEP MY TOES ON ME!

You should try these cigars because . . . they couldn't improve its perfect blend to PLEASE MEN MORE, so they lowered its price to PLEASE MORE MEN.

19. SLOGANIZED ENDING

Even if a statement contains no other device or special theme, it will be more impressive it you can make it terminate with an attractive slogan.

> I changed to Chase & Sanborn Coffee because . . . its unfailing freshness makes it so flavorful that I can actually use less coffee per cup than other brands—PLEASING BOTH PURSE AND PALATE.

> I prefer Jergens Lotion because . . . being extra sensitive, my hands require extra protection—which I find only in this soothing lotion that for so many years has been my STAND-BY HAND-BUY.

> I like Betty Crocker Split Pea Soup because . . . easy in preparation, thrifty in price, and delicious in taste, it helps me to SAVE AS I SERVE.

20. TRIADS

*Tria*d construction—"three of a kind"—seems to be a magical method for winning statement contests. You will find this fortunate formula used as the basis of many entry examples given in this chapter, even when some other special device predominates. Probably the most effective form of triad is built solely upon sales points describing three separate advantages of the product.

> I like Redi-Meat because . . . its waste-free, meal-flattering, flavor-fine goodness—together with its ever-readiness, energizing nourishment and absolute purity—make it our family's daily favorite.

> I like Shurfine Coffee because . . . its cheery fragrance, vigorous flavor, and undeniable thriftiness give a welcome life to lagging spirits, simple meals and pinched budgets.

> New Kix Cereal appeals to me because . . . vitalized to aid health, triple-packed to assure crispness, uniquely formed to add attraction, Kix is our morning delicacy and our all-day body builder.

21. VARIED COMBINATIONS

Pepsi-Cola hits the spot because ... as a quick "lift," it's TOPS to the bottle BOTTOM—first in flavor, first in zest, and first in the hearts of thirsty budgeteers. (*Contrast, Parody*)

I like to wear Thom McAn shoes because ... it is the LAST word in shoemanship that puts them FIRST—and the FIRST word in craftsmanship that makes them LAST. (*Contrast, Double Meaning*)

I use only Cooper Razor Blades because ... there's NO pull, NO nicks, NO scrapes with Cooper—so I KNOW it has the "EDGE" on all other razor blades. (*Alliteration, Repetition, Double Meaning*)

Insist on Champion Spark Plugs because ... with just a taste of gas for SMOOTH-AS-CREAM starts that won't MILK battery life, Champions save STARTING SECONDS and SECOND STARTINGS. (*Analogy, Reversal, Sloganized Ending*)

I like Wish-Bone Italian Dressing because ... today's BEST DRESSED salads WEAR IT PROUDLY—a light, ingenious COATING that brings out unrivalled full flavor, SUITING the most fastidious tastes sublimely, FITTINGLY, properly. (*Analogy, Personification*).

I like Royal Crown Cola because ... it HITS the TOP in quality—HITS the BOTTOM in cost—and what a HIT it makes with my family for genuine enjoyment and economy! (*Contrast, Repetition, Balanced Benefits*)

22. VERSIFICATION

See the next chapter for complete coverage of this widely used winning technique for statement contests.

What Kind of Entries to Submit

In many of the preceding entry examples, there are elements of contrived cleverness. But some are relatively simple, and seem to rely on plain-spoken sincerity to tell how the contest product solved a particular problem or personal situation. While the latter approach is not exactly a device, it is nonetheless a distinct method of entry composition.

How can you tell whether the judges will prefer tricky techniques or simple systems of expression? The truth is, no one can possibly know in advance precisely what kind of entries will win in any particular case—especially in the field of statements—since different types have often won in the very same contest.

Your best bet, therefore, is to *send in as many good entries as possible*—using various methods, from the simplest to the trickiest you can devise. Most contests permit—or even encourage—submission of multiple entries. In rare cases where only one entry is allowed, try for *unique cleverness*—which appeals to most judges, most of the time.

How to Achieve Originality

There is another big advantage in composing as many entries as you can on a given subject: The more you write, the greater will be your chance of achieving that all-important quality in winning entries—ORIGINALITY.

Merely copying and submitting what other entrants have created—as revealed in this book or elsewhere—will benefit nobody, since top judges of national contests are generally familiar with previous winning entries which captured major prizes.

By all means, utilize as many of the methods presented here as you can adapt for whatever contests you enter—but never repeat the exact wording of any published entry. Instead, use these examples to stimulate your own thinking along similar lines. Start jotting down every idea about the contest product or subject that comes to mind; and your compositions will increase in originality as you continue.

Unless you get a sudden stroke of inspiration—which seldom happens to anybody—the first few entries you write on any topic will be rather commonplace, containing obvious ideas occurring to countless other entrants. But, *as you keep on writing*, you'll find your run-of-the-mill thoughts being supplanted by sparkling new notions.

It's something like turning on a garden hose. At first, only stale water will trickle out from its coils—but then, as the flow grows stronger, it gushes forth in a fresh, clear, and steady stream.

So, keep your mental tap turned on full force to produce a flood of original ideas that will sweep your entries toward success.

Chapter 8

HOW TO WIN STATEMENT CONTESTS—IN VERSE

When asked to define the difference between prose and verse, a student replied:

> "There was a young lady named Lee
> Who waded out up to her ankle ...

"That's prose. If she'd gone a little farther, it would have been verse."

Many contestants who start to work on prose statements go a little farther and wind up with statements in verse. *Do such rhymed entries win the approval of most contest judges?* Indeed they do!—and in so many cases that a separate chapter on rhymed statements seems warranted.

Jingles Attract Judges

Merely by its physical appearance, the rhymed form seems to stand out and say "Read me—I'm different!" Its brief lines, wide margins, capital initials, and symmetrical arrangement all bid for attention.

The contest judge, wearied perhaps by a succession of dull entries couched in ordinary prose, will perk up at the sight of your novel stanza, will pause to scan it more closely—and your struggle for recognition is half won! Only *half* won, though, for your verse must be distinctive in content as well as in form, if it is to bring you a prize.

Forms to Follow

When employing verse to finish a statement in the usually required "25 words or less," you will find that a quatrain or four-line jingle generally allows enough room for you to express your ideas fully without exceeding the word limit. That's one reason why most rhymed statements are in quatrain form.

Another reason is that a great deal of popular verse—which contesters naturally tend to imitate—is written in this style, exemplified in the simple but catchy rhythm of "Mary's Lamb." The cadence of this familiar jingle is indicated by capitalized words and syllables to show natural emphasis; while the number at the end of each line tells how many heavy beats or strong accents it contains:

> MA-ry HAD a LIT-tle LAMB   (4)
> Its FLEECE was WHITE as SNOW   (3)
> And EV-ery-WHERE that MA-ry WENT   (4)
> The LAMB was SURE to GO   (3)

When following the pattern of "Mary's Lamb," you may vary the number of syllables in each line to some extent; but there should always be *four* strong beats (emphasized words or syllables) in the first and third lines, and *three* strong beats in the second and fourth lines—with the accent falling on alternate syllables. Much published light verse fits this formula, as in this stanza defining a quatrain itself.

> A quatrain is a four-line rhyme
> That's never out of place—
> It may be used at any time
> To fill an empty space.

"Mary" Often Takes a Prize

While quatrains occasionally fill empty spaces at the bottom of magazine pages, they're even better at filling empty pockets with prize money for entrants who use them skillfully in statement contests. To acquire such skill, study these examples of rhymed four-line entries completing specific statements in the style of "Mary's Lamb":

I prefer Libby's tomato juice because . . .

> Never weak or watered out,
> But always rich and ripe;
> Delicious, clear, and healthful, too—
> Pure Libby's is my type!

75

I like Kool-Aid because . . .

> In coolers for a camping treat,
> Refreshing when we rest,
> It makes our outdoor fun complete
> 'Cause flavor's "Berry Best!"

Yuban coffee is best because . . .

> For flavor, freshness, fragrance fine,
> It's Yuban you should choose;
> For it's the tempting beverage
> That ends all coffee blues.

I prefer to save in a savings bank because . .

> My money is respected there,
> No matter what amount;
> I'm treated like a millionaire,
> Though small is my account.

I like Stuhmer's pumpernickel because . . .

> My children's tastes are often fickle,
> And hubby's hard to please;
> Yet Stuhmer's wholesome pumpernickel
> Suits all with equal ease.

I use Fitch shampoo because . . .

> I find that Fitch will keep my hair
> In healthiest condition—
> So lustrous, neat, attractive, too,
> And always in position.

I prefer Gold Crest mayonnaise because . . .

> This mayonnaise deserves my thanks
> And prompts me to rejoice—
> For Gold Crest dressing always ranks
> The first in family choice.

Looking over these entries, you'll notice that in some cases the jingle's first line rhymes with its third line (as in the last stanza); but in *every* example the second and fourth lines rhyme—as they must in all jingles that follow the general pattern of "Mary's Lamb."

There is, however, another popular form of quatrain, with a rhyme scheme used even more frequently for finishing contest statements. In this other variety of four-line verse, the first line rhymes with the second; and the third line rhymes with the fourth. It might be called the "Twinkle Star" style, after this well-known model:

> Twinkle, Twinkle, little star,
> How I wonder what you are,
> Up above the world so high,
> Like a diamond in the sky.

In each line of this memorable little poem, the accent falls naturally on words or syllables in 1-3-5-7 order. But, if you were to change the beginning of each line only slightly, its rhythmic beat would fall just as naturally into 2-4-6-8 order, like this:

> Oh, TWIN-kle, TWIN-kle, LIT-tle STAR,
> You MAKE me WON-der WHAT you ARE,
> A-WAY a-BOVE the WORLD so HIGH,
> You're LIKE a DIA-mond IN the SKY.

In its original meter or with this minor variation in rhythm, the "Twinkle Star" pattern may be found in countless rhymed statements, since it's the easiest form of verse to compose. Why? Because this model actually consists of two couplets, if you consider the first two lines and the second two lines as separate pairs—and a couplet is the simplest basic rhyming form. Here are several examples on typical commercial topics in "Twinkle Star" style:

I like Boscul coffee because . . .

> Fragrant Boscul, steaming hot,
> Glorifies the coffee pot,
> Adding zest to every meal
> With its appetite appeal.

I like Spry best for all baking and frying because . . .

> Now hasty baking is no trick,
> For Spry blends easy, sure and quick;
> Gives smokeless frying, free from waste,
> And leaves no greasy after-taste.

I like the six-bottle carton of Pepsi-Cola because . . .

> Built to last for safety first,
> Snug-held contents banish thirst;
> Stores away and handles well,
> Thrifty price makes savings swell.

I like Woodbury's soap best for my skin because . . .

> To tell the simple, honest truth,
> It helps retain the bloom of youth,
> Which would have vanished, I'm afraid,
> Except for Woodbury's fine aid.

Campbell tomato juice is best because . . .

> First in color, first in taste,
> Garden goodness without waste,
> Great for drinking, soups or stews—
> This red-white can bans budget blues.

I like the Eversharp-Schick Injector best because . . .

> For shaving comfort, speed and ease,
> The Schick Injector sure does please;
> With no loose parts to go astray,
> It saves me bother every day.

I wear Goodall Palm Beach suits because . . .

> Palm Beach suits are "good all" ways.
> Cool and smart for summer days;
> Quickly cleaned and low prices, too—
> Despite long wear, they look like new.

I prefer Sperry pancake flour because . . .

> With cost so low and value high,
> For better breakfasts I rely
> On Sperry's special finer flour
> For pancake treats my kids devour!

By following either the "Twinkle Star" or "Mary's Lamb" pattern, you can finish any statement in creditable verse. Remember, though, that composing your entry in jingle form—no matter how perfect its rhyme and rhythm—will not automatically make it a winner in a commercial contest. Your versified statement must still contain sound sales points, describing specific advantages of the product or benefits derived from its use.

Adding Sparkle to Your Stanzas

Most of the techniques demonstrated in Chapters 6 and 7 for creating limerick last lines and prose entries can be applied to statements in verse, like this one using color words and inner rhyme:

I like Shinola White Cleaner because . . .

> When dingy SHOES give me the BLUES,
> And budget's near the RED,
> Shinola WHITE makes shoes look RIGHT
> And saves "long GREEN" instead.

Parody and double meaning are effectively employed to complete this statement: I like Shurfine shortening because . . .

> Home, home, by the RANGE,
> Where I gave Shurfine shortening a test
> There never is heard a dissatisfied word—
> For it proved undeniably best!

A clever pun on "a la carte" helped this jingle win a statement contest about Pepsi-Cola's six-bottle carton:

> It's easy to buy a big supply;
> Our budget we're outsmartin'—
> Thrift and thirst we satisfy
> With Pepsi "a la carton!"

Contrast was twice brought into play to tell why this entrant likes iced tea:

> When the temperature's HIGH
> And my energy's LOW,
> A glass of Iced Tea
> Makes my "STOP" turn to "GO"!

Related Words and Homonyms are exemplified in this entry on "Why we should all support the March of Dimes":

> By ADDING our MITE to this parade,
> We MULTIPLY the MIGHT of medical aid,

79

DIVIDE the costs that must be paid,
SUBTRACT the sacrifices made.

Analogy is used in this jingle, finishing the statement: I like Baby Ruth candy because ...

When lagging pep has me AT SEA
And I don't feel like action,
Rich Baby Ruth restores me with
A RAFT of satisfaction.

An acrostic in rhyme is somewhat harder to compose within the 25-word limit; but here are two well-done examples:

I enjoy *Grit Magazine* because ...

G ood, clean stories make a hit—
R estful reading—welcome wit—
I nterest in every bit—
T hat's why I'm so fond of GRIT!

I like Spry best for all baking and frying because ...

S ince I've used it faithfully,
P a and kids have praise for me;
R elishing my pies and fries,
"Y our cooking's great!" they harmonize.

When Longer Letters Are Allowed

While most contest statements are limited to 25 words, some competitions call for letters on a given topic up to 100 words. When rules allow such leeway, the rhyme-minded contestant can really go to town. Greater wordage naturally permits wider range of expression, as well as a variety of poetic forms other than the familiar quatrain.

Judges of longer letter contests seem to favor rhymed entries— probably because a lengthy prose missive may make rather dull reading, while sprightly verse can enliven almost any subject, as the following examples will show.

When Pillsbury invited contestants to tell, in 100 words or less, why they liked Sno Sheen cake flour in a new package with a built-in sifter, one winner used this attractive lyrical style:

What could be handier,
Finer or dandier,
Than Sno Sheen, so cleverly packed?
Its measuring sifter
Is such a task lifter—
I think it's a wonder, in fact!

No waste and no worry,
No bother or flurry,
Are known when I use this device.
It assures proper sifting
In one simple shifting,
And measures are always precise.

It banishes guesswork,
Makes baking much less work,
Without any fuss or mistakes.
Its value is double,
For it saves time and trouble,
And helps me produce perfect cakes.

In another contest of *unlimited* wordage on "Why I Like Oakite for Cleaning," the same poetic pattern proved successful. As in the Sno Sheen verses, each of the following six-line stanzas uses a rhyme scheme know as a-a-b-c-c-b. That is, lines 1 and 2 rhyme (a-a); lines 4 and 5 rhyme (c-c); and line 3 rhymes with line 6 (b-b)—which results in a pleasing rhythmic effect.

For cleaning my sink
And bathroom, I think
That Oakite cannot be matched.
It makes them so white,
So gleamingly bright,
And never leaves anything scratched.

It's sure a fine friend
On which to depend,
As I've found by its regular use.
It serves me each day
In many a way
Toward keeping my home neat and spruce.

But what I like most

Is the way I can coast
Through my cleaning with Oakite's great aid.
I need no strong arm,
For it works like a charm—
All thanks to the way it is made.

No more need I scrub
To clean sink or tub;
I'm rid of that back-breaking plight.
Now it's all just a lark,
For, I'm glad to remark,
When Oakite arrives, dirt takes flight!

Effective Expression

Another excellent model to follow when writing poems for letter contests is the rondeau. This is a fixed form of 15 lines, with only two different rhymes used throughout 13 lines, plus two short un-rhymed refrain lines.

While a rondeau is not easy to compose, it is especially effective for expressing one dominant idea or theme. Its rhyming style is equally suitable for subjects in a light or serious vein, as shown in the two following examples created by the author of this book for contests which had called only for "letters."

The first required 100 words or less on "What I Would Do With a Tax-free Million-Dollar Gift." Published results of this contest revealed that some winners considered the problem quite earnestly—but not in this case:

A Million Bucks! If I could show
A tax-free pile of that much dough,
    My frugal ways I'd put aside
    And take my family for a ride
To Florida where sunbeams glow.

I cannot say how things will go,
But I would want to have it so—
    If some kind fate would just provide
        A Million Bucks.

We'd buy an ocean-front chateau
Upon Miami Beach, you know,
   And there, in happiness and pride,
   We all would ritzily abide . . .
At least, that is, until we blow
      A Million Bucks!

A more serious note was struck by this entry in rondeau form, submitted on the subject, "Why I Want to See the New York World's Fair":

The future, fair and bright and gay,
With all its marvelous array,
   Is here revealed in imagery
   Full fashioned out of Time To Be—
Tomorrow's world on view today.

Once seen, it holds us in its sway
So that, no sooner we're away,
   Again we feel the lure to see
      The future Fair.

For here alone can we survey
A peaceful world at work and play—
   A symbol of a land that's free
   And of its brilliant destiny,
To show us all how brightly may
      The Future fare.

Acrostics Stand Out

If rondeaus seem too highly stylized for your taste in rhymed composition, and you still wish to achieve an outstanding effect with versified letters, you can try an acrostic poem, such as the following entry in Walter Winchell's contest for 50 words or less on the topic, "Why I Could Never Be a Communist."

> *C* ancelling civilized rules,
> *O* ut to make mankind their tools;
> *M* alicious, vicious, and vile,
> *M* asters of menace and guile;
> *U* ngodly, unfeeling, unjust,
> *N* otorious breakers of trust;
> *I* mmoral corruptors of youth,
> *S* atanic distorters of truth;
> *T* reacherous, cruel in creed—
> *S* uch is the Communist breed!

On quite a different theme—"What the United States Means to Me"—This excellent entry won with a rhymed acrostic.

> *U* pon the surface of this earth
> *N* o land can equal ours.
> *I* t gives to every man of worth
> *T* he chance to prove his powers—
> *E* xcluding none by creed or birth,
> *D* enying none its dowers.
>
> *S* uch precious liberty is rare
> *T* oday in other lands;
> *A* nd so we find it doubly fair—
> *T* his gift Columbia hands
> *E* xtended for us all to share,
> *S* o long as Freedom stands.

The two preceding examples of acrostic verse happen to be more literary than commercial; but this form of entry is often successful in letter contests about typical consumer products, such as this one on "Why I Like Pepsodent Tooth Paste":

> *P* ure and pleasing to the taste,
> *E* ffective, safe, and free from waste,
> *P* epsodent's my choice tooth paste.
> *S* teady use each day and night
> *O* f Pepsodent will keep teeth white,
> *D* evoid of film and gleaming bright.
> *E* xtra value for what's spent
> *N* ever caused me discontent—
> *T* hat's why I like Pepsodent!

Another form of rhymed acrostic is exemplified by this winner, on the subject "Why I Prefer Armstrong Quaker Rugs":

> *Q* is for Quality in the name that they bear;
> *U* is for Use—they are famed for long wear;
> *A* is for Admirable style and design;
> *K* is for Keenness in every smart line;
> *E* is for Ease in keeping them clean;
> *R* is for Richness that's fit for a queen.

> Put them together and they will spell QUAKER—The finest of rugs—for Armstrong's the maker!

When submitting acrostic entries—whether in prose or verse—you should make the initials which form the vertical words stand out in some way to attract attention. This can be done by underlining, separating, or enlarging the key letters, or by writing them in a color different from the rest of your entry.

Victory Via Verse

In the first part of this chapter, the quatrain style of "Mary's Lamb" was advocated as a model for short statements in verse. The same simple pattern may be used for longer letters by making each "paragraph" a four-line stanza. Here is such a winning entry on the theme "What 'Great Expectations' Do You Have for Your Child?"

> A Scientist beloved by all,
>   I'd want my son to be—
> A benefactor of the world,
>   To aid humanity.

> Perhaps he may invest some way
>   To make man's burden less;
> Or find a cure that's quick and sure
>   To help those in distress.

> "Great Expectations," these, I know;
>   But that is what I plan—
> To have my boy bring world-wide joy
>   By benefitting Man!

Whatever poetic pattern you prefer to use for your own entries, you may confidently expect to be well rewarded for expressing your letters and statements in rhymed form—since it is a proved fact in this field that vivid verse can lead to victory.

Chapter 9

HOW TO WIN NAME CONTESTS

At first glance, a contest to make up a name appears to offer the easiest way to win a prize. After all, a name generally consists of only one or two words—perhaps three, at most. What could be simpler?

That's how it may seem to one who approaches a naming contest without previous experience in this field. However, in actual practice, it takes considerable skill, study, and effort to compose successful entries for such competitions.

While naming contests may entail a good deal of preparatory work, there can be no question about their lavish generosity to winning entrants. On a money-per-word basis, sponsors of name contests have awarded some of the largest prizes ever paid—such as $25,000 for the single word "Majorette" as a flower name. Other awards of $20,000 and $10,000 each for one lone word have been made; while prizes of $5,000 for single names are customary in this particular kind of contest.

At this point, some distinction should be made between "names" and "titles" as applied to different contest categories in this book, although those terms are often used interchangeably. When appellations of not more than three words are required for any person, animal, object, product, service, symbol, or the like, they are considered "names." Longer appellations—especially intended for cartoons and pictures—are designated "titles" or "captions"–and are covered in the next chapter.

Seek the Right Slant

In virtually every naming contest, the rules state that entries will be judged on the basis of aptness and originality. Therefore, these two standards should be considered of paramount importance when composing your name entries.

To score high in aptness, the names you submit must fit the *specific* nature of the contest subject. For example, if you were told only to name a bull, it would be quite fitting to use a word suggesting ferocity or brute strength. But, if the contest announcement described the bull as a meek, flower-sniffing specimen of the "Ferdinand" type, an entirely different slant would be required to make your entry appropriate. Aptness, then, could be achieved with *wild* words or *mild* words—depending on whether your subject was "terri-bull" or "affa-bull."

To be *original*, your names must not be *obvious*. When Bon Ami ran a contest to name its famous trademark—the newly hatched chick that "hasn't scratched yet"— thousands of unthinking entrants took their cue from the product's own name and submitted "Bonnie." While not wholly lacking in aptness, such duplicated entries were entirely devoid of originality and had no chance whatsoever of winning.

Bon Ami's first prize—a $10,000 diamond ring symbolizing the company's 75th anniversary—was reportedly awarded for "Impecka Bill." This name was not only appropriate for both the subject (a chick) and the product (an "impeccable" cleanser) but it was outstandingly original—with a difference in conception and expression that won the judges' highest favor.

Birth of a Notion

How do you think a top prize winning name like "Impecka Bill" came into being? You can be sure it did not occur spontaneously to the Bon Ami winner. In all likelihood, this wise contestant followed a method which any name-seeking entrant can pursue with a good chance of ultimate success.

To take the first step in this name-creating system, you must compile various lists of words pertaining to all phases of the subject under consideration. Thus, if you had been working on the Bon Ami Chick-naming contest, your classified lists might look something like this:

CHICK-RELATED WORDS

shell . . . hatch . . . crack . . . coop . . . lay . . . egg . . .
hen . . . rooster . . . poultry . . . fowl . . . feathers . . .
bird . . . down . . . peck . . . cackle . . . scratch . . .
peep . . . cheep . . . barn . . . crow . . . bill . . . beak . . .
yellow . . . yolk . . . fluffy . . . chicken feed . . . paltry sum.

PRODUCT-RELATED WORDS

safe . . . scratchless . . . sparkle . . . polish . . . soft . . .
fast . . . gentle . . . mild . . . smooth . . . clean . . .
sanitary . . . easy . . . efficient . . . speedy . . . thrifty . . .
spotless . . . flawless . . . perfect . . . faultless . . . impeccable.

Many such words can be drawn from your own mind, by the process of thought association. If they don't come readily enough, you can look for related terms in a dictionary or thesaurus. Searching for synonyms that way would inevitably turn up "impeccable," which has the same meaning as "perfect" or "faultless."

By comparing your two lists, you'll soon note that "impeccable" is a sort of chain word, linking together the sounds of "peck" and "bill." So you break the chain apart and come up with an exceptionally apt and original name—IMPECKA BILL—which is probably how the Bon Ami winner did it.

Successful Naming Systems

Compiling word lists to work with is an absolute *must* for every naming contest. They provide the raw material which you can design, refine, and combine into novel creations that will make the judges appreciate your efforts.

However, the Bon Ami demonstration is by no means the only method for coining new names from old words. Following are several other naming systems which have won innumerable prizes in the past—and can win for *you* if properly applied to present and future contests.

ALLITERATION

Since alliteration means using the same starting sound, it is most effective in names of two or three words, such as these:

Blushing Belle	Fast Flying Flash
Java Joy	Golden Girl Gloves
Lady Littlecost	Handy Home Helper
Magic Mould	Quick Carrot Cubes
Tasty Treats	Super Speed Streamliner

However, even a single word can be alliterative if it contains syllables beginning with the same sound, as:

daydream	nearness	seaside	daffodil
fanfare	puppet	tiptop	lavaliere
mermaid	ramrod	zigzag	temptation

ANALOGY

Simply defined, analogy describes something in terms of something else. When the Kennedy administration was called The New Frontier, that was a form of analogy. So was the appellation Sultan of Swat for Babe Ruth and Brown Bomber for Joe Louis. Here are some other names of this kind, with their subjects, as used in contests:

auto: Road Rocket
bicycle: Arrow Flight
cruise ship: Magic Carpet
health food: Dynamo Power
plane: Shooting Star

race horse: Lightning Flash
rose bush: Ember Glow
train: Silver Meteor
typewriter: Hummingbird
white cake: Snow Topper

COMBINATION

More names are coined by combination than by any other single system. In its most elementary form, it is accomplished by linking two words that end or begin with the same letter, as in these examples:

Butteroyal (butter + royal)
Glamourobe (glamour + robe)
Heraldawn (herald + dawn)
Guardoor (guard + door)
Loyalad (loyal + lad)

Realemon (real + lemon)
Smartog (smart + tog)
Reveland (revel + land)
Sweetaste (sweet + taste)
Ultrabode (ultra + abode)

A slight variation of this technique is to join words with a double-letter connection:

Bestarch (best + starch)
Polisheen (polish + sheen)

Richarm (rich + charm)
Youthrill (youth + thrill)

More advanced among merging methods—and more effective in winning prizes—is "syllablending," which itself is a coined name for the process of syllable blending. These entries demonstrate how this technique works:

beautility (beauty + utility)

holidaisy (holiday + daisy)

invitamin (invite + vitamin)

medalicious (medal + delicious)

miraclean (miracle + clean)

orangelic (orange + angelic)

petalure (petal + allure)

regallant (regal + gallant)

shoppertunity (shopper + opportunity)

ultimotor (ultimate + motor)

"Coining by joining" was developed into a fine art by the late Walter Winchell. Here are just a few of WW's most picturesque "combinamings":

femmedian	New Yorchids
infanticipate	New Yorkitecture
Hollywoodarling	splituation
lasstronaut	swelegant

Still another way to create a new name is to combine the first syllables or initials from words relating to the product or sponsor. Some well-known brand names coined in this manner include NABISCO from National Biscuit Company, PALCO from Pacific Lumber Company, and AMOCO from American Oil Company. In contest entries, of course, such obvious combinations should be avoided. Rather, use syllables from some apt phrase of your own composition. For example, you might name a product "PLEVAL"—explaining briefly that it was derived from "*PL*ease *EV*erybody *AL*ways."

A final variation does not actually combine words in the sense of merging or blending, but merely puts two unchanged words together to make a single descriptive term, as in these names:

Brewmaster	Fleetfoot	Newstyle
Coppercoat	Goldentart	Strongheart
Easycare	Markwell	Thriftway

EXTENSION

In this method you add an extra syllable or two as a suffix to change a word's sound, meaning, or appearance. Suffixes that may readily be used include:

-ade	-eer	-ic	-ode
-all	-elle	-ine	-ola
-ama	-esque	-ique	-oma
-are	-ette	-ity	-ona
-ate	-ex	-ize	-ore

By adding such suffixes to ordinary words, winning names like these have been composed:

Coolerama	Medality	Scarletelle
Jewelette	Nuggetine	Tropicola
Lemonique	Opalesque	Velvetex

PARODY

Next to the combination system, the technique of parody is probably most successful in naming contests. For convenience in utilizing this method, you should compile or acquire lists of names that are famous in history, music, literature, or any well-known field. You should also possess a collection of ordinary masculine and feminine first names. Both types—notable and commonplace—may be effectively parodied so long as their original form remains recognizable.

The name of Sir Lancelot, most renowned of King Arthur's knights, has been parodied in more contests than any other famed appellation. Here are some winning versions, with the objects to which they applied:

acrobat: Sir Bouncelot	goat: Sir Munchalot
clown: Sir Laughsalot	hypnotist: Sir Trancelot
dog: Sir Pantsalot	mule: Sir Lagsalot
farmer: Sir Plantsalot	parrot: Sir Chatsalot
gladiator: Sir Stanchalot	pony: Sir Prancelot

You will readily recognize other famous names which have been parodied by the following entries:

Cleocatra (cat)	Home Tweet Home (bird house)
Dobbinhood (pony)	Hopalong Sassily (kangaroo)
Eiffel Towser (French poodle)	Newtopia (home)
Garden of Eatin' (restaurant)	Prints Charming (dress)
Gay Travelero (auto)	Sir Walter Roarly (lion)
Ghouldilocks (gorilla)	Wee Huskiteers (twin babies)
Hiawoofa (puppy)	Wizard of "Ahs" (chef)

Take-offs on common personal names include such entries as these:

| Charlequin (pony) | Hambrose (pig) | Shortimer (dachshund) |
| Gemily (doll) | Pranklin (monkey) | Tabigail (kitten) |

RHYME

Old Gold and *Pall Mall*, well-known cigarette brands, are typical of rhyming names used by many popular products. The same device has won countless prizes in naming contests, as shown by these samples:

Airy Dairy	Gay Way	Quick Stick
Clean Queen	Handy Dandy	Rest Best
Date Bait	Kill Chill	Swing King

Here, again, your lists of subject-related words should prove a fruitful source of possible rhymes. If, for example, you were trying to name a space ship or rocket, your reference list should soon suggest such rhyming names as: Space Ace, Higher Flyer, Star Car, Fission Mission, Globe Probe, Wander Yonder, and Lunar Communer.

If rhymes do not occur to you readily when going over your word lists, consult a rhyming dictionary—which should be a standard part of your contesting equipment. (See Chapter 13, Sources of Success.)

SEPARATION

This technique is the exact opposite of combination. Instead of putting words together, you take them apart. An excellent example of separation was given at the start of this chapter in the Bon Ami first prize winning chick name, "Impecka Bill," derived by dividing "impeccable."

To create names by this method, you should first make a special list of polysyllabic words relating to your subject. Then experiment with these terms until you find some which can be split into the most likely names.

To demonstrate this system once more, as was done with the Bon Ami contest, suppose you had to rename Santa Claus. Descriptive words in your list might include: altruist, amiable, benevolent, benign, bountiful, cheerful, donation, festive, generous, genial, hilarious, indulgent, jocular, jolly, jovial, liberal, mirthful, munificent, and philanthropic.

Simply by splitting some of these words apart, you could devise such fitting names for Santa Claus as: Al Truist, Ben Evolent, Don Nation, Gene Nial, Hy Larious, Jo Cular, and Phil N. Thropic.

SPONSOR SLANT

Though most naming contests are commercially sponsored, their subjects do not always lend themselves to use of the sponsor's or product's own name in entries. However, you might try to work in some such reference whenever it seems fitting to do so. Since many other entrants may get similar ideas, you should attempt to apply this method in a different and distinctive way.

This unique approach was well exemplified in a sandwich-naming contest sponsored by Swift's canned meat, Prem. Top prize of $1,000 was awarded for "Major Premway"—which dignified the product with an impressive title that was at the same time a clever pun on the phrase "made your Prem way." Lesser winners in this contest also used sponsor-slanted or product-praising names, such as Prema Donna, Premsation, and Swift SuPREMacy.

Once in a while, though, the simplest sort of sponsor appeal will put an entry in front. When auto-maker Henry J. Kaiser ran a contest to find a name for his new line of cars, first prize went for— "Henry J"!

WORD PLAY

This final category is the broadest of all—it includes puns, double meaning, reversal, spelling tricks, and similar devices.

A classic example of double-meaning word play in a first prize winning name is "Gypsy Roundelayer." This entry won $5,000 in a Gold Medal contest to name a spicy chocolate cake. The word "gypsy" described the cake's dark allure; while "roundelayer" not only applied to its appearance (round layer) but suggested the recurring appeal of a gypsy melody or *roundelay*.

"Sudsabelle" won the top award of $20,000 as a name for Swan soap's ad character, Mama Swan. In this specimen of word play, the spelling of "sudsable" was changed slightly to give that term a feminine slant fitting both subject and product.

"Seaquarium" was another first prize contest name (now used for the far-famed marine exhibit in Miami) which could be construed in two ways—as "see" or "sea" aquarium. In addition to its double meaning, this name also exemplifies the art of combination. Major winners in this field, as you will observe, generally employ more than one minting method.

Other forms of word play have been used to coin names for the following wide variety of subjects—some of which would fit equally well under the parody classification, since there is considerable overlapping in these categories.

auto: Joyager
beverage: N-R-G
bicycle: Pumpanion
boat: Spunky Dory
bungalow: Happinest
cow: Miss Americow
dog: Barkaneer
fishing rod: Aristocast
jaywalker: Otto Knowbetter
lion: Emperoar
mansion: Muchtoo Lodge
metal: My-T-Lite

mustang: Bronc's Cheer
percolator: Driplomat
perfume: Scentsation
pony: Trottentot
puppy: Wagabond
race horse: Winspuration
rug: Persianality
space monkey: Baboom
space station: Blast Office
speeder: Fillmore Graves
teakettle: Mother's Whistler
watch: Wristocrat

SUMMARY

To sum up the preceding advice on coining names, you should always follow these three points:

1. Make extensive lists of words relating to the subject.

2. Consider standard names or terms in common usage that can be changed to fit your needs.

3. Use one or more of the naming methods described in this chapter.

Chapter 10

HOW TO WIN CAPTION CONTESTS

In this chapter, the words "caption" and "title" will be used interchangeably, as they are in most contests of this general nature. Rarely is any distinction made between those two terms by judges who consider entries in this field.

Some contestants may believe that a title describes a picture, photo or cartoon, while a caption quotes what an illustrated character is saying. But, often as not, those designations may be transposed in relation to the definitions given. Therefore, you may interpret them either way, depending upon specific contest rules for proper meaning and usage.

The one thing that most caption or title contests have in common is a picture on which they are based. This may vary from a rough sketch or cartoon to an elaborate photograph in natural color. But the picture's composition is of little matter, for its entire significance to contestants is in its *subject*.

What sort of subjects are used for picture-titling contests? Sometimes they relate to the sponsor's product or service; but in other cases they have no connection at all with the sponsor's business. Both types will be fully described here for your guidance.

Current Topics

To foster better ways of using electricity in the home, industries represented by Edison Electric Institute sponsored a "Housepower" contest, offering $100,000 worth of prizes. It called for captions of 15 words or less for a cartoon depicting a middle-aged man and wife in this night-time bedroom scene:

Clad in pajamas, the husband is sitting on the edge of a twin bed, looking baffled and bewildered. His nightgowned wife in the other bed is watching him with mixed sympathy and disapproval. He is evidently trying to figure out where to connect a portable television set. Apparently the room has only one wall outlet, feeding triple socket plugs from which tangled wires lead to a clock, radio, percolator, electric blankets, and several lamps. No outlet or extension is available for the TV set; and even if it could be connected instead of another appliance, it would drain off power from all the rest and reduce its own efficiency (as explained in advertisements and entry blanks for this contest).

That's the situation for which contestants had to find suitable captions. *How did they go about it?* They used the same procedure applicable to almost every kind of creative contest—making lists of appropriate words for the given subject. In this case, electrical terms like these were most fitting:

amplify	connect	generate	plug
appliance	consume	glow	power
blow out	cord	hook up	shock
bright	current	juice	short
bulb	cut off	light	socket
burn out	dynamo	line	switch
capacity	electrify	load	turn on
charge	extension	ohm	volt
circuit	fixture	outlet	watt
conduct	fuse	overload	wire

Typical Titles

From such lists, "Housepower" entrants derived key words on which they based the following captions, typifying the slant that proved most successful in this contest:

1. As Western Union says, "To avoid disappointment, WIRE ahead!"
2. CURRENT events just aren't up to date around here.
3. Don't you know that those OUTLETS are just *inlets* for trouble?
4. Full Housepower would eliminate this SHOCKING SWITCH-uation!
5. Mother, can you spare a LINE?
6. Never overestimate the POWER of your house.
7. Remember—a SWITCH in time saves LINE!
8. Till we're better wired, *turning in* is safer than TURNING ON!

9. WATT'S the reason we can't SWITCH to full Housepower for ELECTRIFYING results?
10. You see—over-EXTENSION always leaves insufficient CURRENT-cy!

These entries, you will note, employ devices described in previous chapters of this book. *Double meaning* and *puns* are used in captions 1, 2, 4 and 9. *Contrast* and *similarity* appear in numbers 3 and 8, while number 10 *combines a pun with analogy*.

Parody is effectively used in the other three captions, as you will recognize. Number 5 is based on the song title, "Brother, Can You Spare a Dime;" number 6, on the magazine slogan, "Never underestimate the power of a woman;" and number 7, on the proverb, "A stitch in time saves nine."

Parody Pays Off

Since parody is one of the most frequently used techniques for composing winning picture titles, you will find great help for such contests in collections of popular expressions, proverbs, advertising phrases, and names of well-known songs, books, movies, plays, and TV programs. Here is just a small sampling of what your parody-source collections should contain:

After the ball is over
Age before beauty
All quiet on the Western
  Front
All wool and a yard wide
Ambassador of good will
Ask the man who owns one
Better late than never
Calling all cars
Century of progress
Charge of the Light
  Brigade
Crime does not pay
Custer's last stand
Desire under the elms
Don't give up the ship

Experience is the best teacher
For whom the bell tolls
Freedom of the seas
Good to the last drop
Hall of fame
Have gun, will travel
Heavens to Betsy
Hit and run
Home on the range
Home sweet home
House that Jack built
How green was my valley
Life begins at 40
Mutiny on the Bounty
Postman always rings twice
Roaming in the gloaming

Shot heard 'round the world	The light that failed
Stop, look, and listen	The power and the glory
Straw that broke the camel's back	There's good news tonight
Tarzan of the apes	Trip the light fantastic
	Wizard of Oz
	Yankee Doodle Dandy

How such source material can be profitably used was well demonstrated by winners of the Colgate contest, which offered prizes worth $200,000 for titling a picture of a famous episode in American history. The scene to be captioned showed Benjamin Franklin flying his kite during a storm, amid heavy rain and flashes of lightning. His kite string carried a key used in his experiment to reveal the electrical nature of lightning.

Leads from Lists

Experienced entrants in this contest, after studying all details depicted, first compiled a list of electrical terms—such as the "Housepower" words given earlier in this chapter—and added other expressions with a scientific and patriotic slant, pertaining directly to the Franklin picture.

These *specific* word lists, considered in conjunction with general collections of familiar terms, brought forth the following winning titles, each employing the art of parody:

Amp-bassador of good skill	Power for men and glory for Ben
Charge of the kite rig aid	Experiment is the best reader
Squall of fame	Tapping the light fantastic
Heavens to Benny!	The short seen 'round the world
Ohming in the gloaming	Yankee did all dandy

Devices other than parody which proved successful in titling the Franklin picture included the following:

Alliteration: Riddle resolving rendezvous
Analogy: Current dividend from a key investment
Coined word: Communikiting with nature

99

Color: Bolt from blue makes red letter day
Contrast: The high sign that gave the lowdown
Double meaning: Founding father in a shocking situation
Homonym: A tale within a tail
Humor: He's nuts about bolts
Pun: And soddenly he saw the light!
Related words: A raisin' that grew into a current
Similarity: From his wits came our watts
Verse: Ben's bolt brings volt

You will notice that several of these winners combined various techniques suitable for this sort of contest. For example, the title "He's nuts about bolts" has humor, double meaning, and related words. Caption contests allow a wide latitude of usable devices; *and you may even kid the subject—so long as it does not refer to the sponsor's product,* which of course is sacrosanct.

Picturing the Product

Puss 'n Boots supplied a good example of a title contest based upon a picture concerning the sponsor's product, advertised as "America's largest-selling cat food."

Ads for this contest featured an attractive, natural-color photograph of a mother cat and four kittens beside a grocery shopping bag from which several cans of Puss 'n Boots have been removed. Looking upward expectantly, the cats appeared to await opening of the cans for their enjoyment.

Here, again, the first step was to list words appropriate for the subject of the picture—not only for the cats shown, but for their favorite food, Puss 'n Boots, like these:

Cat Words

cat	fur	paws	puss
claws	glossy	pet	sleek
coat	kitten	playful	tail
feline	mew	purr	whiskers

appetite	feed	meal	nutrition
can	fish	minerals	pep
diet	growth	natural	protein
energy	health	nourishing	vitamins

These words could be derived directly from the Puss 'n Boots ads, contest blank, and can label, as well as from the entrant's own mind, dictionary, or thesaurus. From such sources, the following titles were composed, using indicated devices:

> There's good MEWS tonight—Puss 'n Boots for cats' delight! (*parody and rhyme*)

> Puss 'n Boots makes all cats stop, look and GLISTEN. (*parody*)

> SLEEK operators corner the Puss 'n Boots market. (*analogy*)

> FISHING for Puss 'n Boots with NATURAL-LURE. (*coined word and analogy*)

> On Puss 'n Boots they solely dine—which keeps them always FELINE fine! (*pun and rhyme*)

Just in Jest

When sponsored by newspapers or magazines, rather than by product manufacturers, cartoon caption contests seek only humorous gag lines. This slant was well illustrated by winners in a contest conducted by the New York *Daily News*, which awarded top prizes for these titles for the cartoons described:

Man with bandaged nose meets friend, who observes: "Well, pal, I see you lost a big nasal battle."

Fat woman on scale, with husband watching. He says: "What you need is mind over platter, dear."

Woman to clerk at perfume counter: "It did drive him mad, but now I only see him on visiting days."

Doctor with medical satchel is buying "Get Well" cards. Observer quips: "It's not in the cards, Doc—it's in the bag."

Little girl, overhearing father's comment on TV actress, asks: "Mommy, isn't an 'eyeful' a tower in France?"

Offering dish-towel to reluctant husband, wife remarks: "It's guaranteed not to shrink from washing—why should you?"

Safety Sayings

Since safety is a recurrent theme in caption contests, you can prepare for coming competitions on this subject by studying some cartoon titles which won prizes from the National Safety Council. Most of them, you will note, contain puns or word play:

Cartoon: Wife smoking in bed, as husband rushes in with fire extinguisher.
Title: "Are you trying to make us FLAMOUS over night?"

Cartoon: Husband is standing on shaky boxes stacked on a chair to fix a ceiling light socket, while wife watches fearfully.
Title: "The RUNG approach would be RIGHT here!"

Cartoon: Supervisor rebuking girl worker with long loose hairdo, as she operates pressing machine.
Title: "A perfect CRIPPLE PLAY—tresses to presses to messes!"

Cartoon: Groom stumbles on loose rug while carrying bride through doorway.
Title: "Is this our TRIP to the FALLS?"

Cartoon: A woman trying to park her car is beaten to the space by a sneaky male driver.
Title: "When you CUT IN, you CUT OUT road safety!"

Cartoon: Mother slips on a child's plaything carelessly left on the floor.
Title: "The SITE of a toy UPSET her."

No lesson on picture titling would be complete without covering the subject most often used—babies. Hundreds of contests, national as well as local, have been based on photos of infants wearing all sorts of expressions—and little else.

Entrants are asked to tell what the pictured baby is supposed to be saying. Winning captions in such contests rarely contain tricky words or devices. They depend mostly on the comic effect of making the tot utter a mature, sophisticated remark that could apply only to the world of adults. Here are some winners showing this slant, based on the baby's described expression, as they appeared in another New York *Daily News* contest:

Tired and displeased, rubbing one eye wearily: "Well, maybe the second act will be better."

Holding rattle aloft with puzzled look: "You mean I was waving this at the office party?"

Indignant attitude: "Yeah, I told off the boss like you said—so I'm home early!"

Smiling coyly: "You must be mistaken, miss. All I whistled for was a cab!"

Frowning in concentration: "Now where did I spend that five?"

Lips twisted in a sneer: "Don't take an inventory of your purse now, lady! Just deposit your bus fare!"

Annoyed appearance: "A little service at this end of the counter, please!"

Rubbing nose disgustedly: "Oh brother, do I need a new gag writer!"

Whether you're composing a title for a simple baby picture or a scene of comparative complexity, remember this prize-winning pointer:

Study the subject until you perceive some special significance in it—then create a caption to convey that significance to the contest judges so vividly that you'll surely be entitled to an award.

Chapter 11

HOW TO WIN SLOGAN CONTESTS

"Today's Big Contest Winners Were Yesterday's Beginners." That's a slogan—and a good one. It's specific, mentioning the subject it covers—contests. It has rhythm—read it aloud and note the swing. It has contrast—"today" and "yesterday." It has rhyme and alliteration—"big winners" and "beginners." It employs effective figures of speech—"today" for present, "yesterday" for past. It is brief, memorable and impressive—once read, it lingers in your mind. And it has the ring of universal truth— for *all* outstanding winners, in every field of endeavor, were at one time only beginners.

You will find some of those characteristics in most prize-winning slogans, along with other distinctive qualities to be considered here. First, however, you should understand the nature and purpose of a slogan, as used in contests and advertising.

A slogan should say a lot in a few words. It may describe the virtues of a product, advise a course of action, or epitomize generally known facts—as in the phrase at the start of this chapter. But whatever its intention, it should be brief, clear, and to the point. A whole lesson on slogan writing could be capsuled into three words: *To sloganize, summarize!*

Naturally, if you want to summarize the essentials of any subject, you must know it quite thoroughly. So the first step in composing slogans—as with other forms of entries—is to become familiar with the contest subject from every source available. Next comes the inevitable compilation of appropriate word lists—a preliminary advocated for all creative contests.

After collecting your basic material, select salient terms that may be woven into striking slogans by using one or more of the winning techniques illustrated here.

You will find these methods much like the ones recommended for creation of contest statements in Chapter 7—which is not surprising, since a slogan is actually a statement stripped of all excess verbiage, boiled down to its essence, refined and reformed into a sparkling new expression that crystallizes a keynote idea.

Successful Slogan Systems

Each slogan exemplifying one of the following techniques has its subject identified, so that you may perceive how effectively the slogan fulfills its purpose.

Many of these examples illustrate more than the single creative method under which they are classified, as indicated in parentheses after such slogans.

ACROSTIC

> Coal: *C* omfort *O* f *A* merican *L* ife
>
> Fish: *F* ish *I* nsures *S* ound *H* ealth

ALLITERATION

> Auto: Best bet's a Buick
>
> Canned corn: Fresh from Flavorland
>
> Florida fashions: Sunny styles for sunny living (*repetition*)
>
> Washer: Most wanted by most women (*repetition*)

ANALOGY

> Cancer fund: Arrest cancer—it's wanted for murder!
>
> Oranges: Live wires need plenty of juice
>
> Wallet: Snug corral for roving bucks

BALANCED PHRASES

> Charity: The most you can give is the least you can do (*contrast*)

Classified ads: Read for profit—use for results

Shortening: Bans smoke and smell—blends fast and well (*rhyme*)

Tomato juice: A stop to thirst—a step to health (*similarity*)

COINED WORDS

Salve: Just the thing for skinjuries

Shoes: More styleage, more mileage, more smileage (*rhyme, repetition, alliteration, triad*)

COLOR WORDS

Department store: Make our silver anniversary your golden shopportunity (*coined word*)

Laundry soap: Makes blue Monday a red letter day for washing

COMPARISON

Moccasins: Like strolling on a cloud

Soap: A soap-clean complexion with cold-cream protection (*rhyme*)

CONTRAST

Flour: Stop making blunders—start baking wonders! (*alliteration, rhyme*)

Freewheeling: The coming way of going places

Gasoline: Travel in high at low cost

Shoes: Outer beauty, inner worth

TV station: The first word in news—the last word in entertainment

DOUBLE MEANING

Auto: Smart as its owner

Peanuts: When hunger drives you nutty—eat Tom's

Tissue: What a material difference!

Underwear: Next to myself I like B.V.D. best

PARODY

Adhesive: It's so nice to have a can around the house

Coffee: Man's best blend

Diapers: Rock-a-dry baby

Doughnuts: What foods these morsels be!

Liquor: It reigns where it pours

Masseur: The paws that refresh

Race track: The greatest show on turf

Shoes: For a Happy Shoe Year

Suntan lotion: Get what you bask for

Toothpaste: A miss is as good as her smile

TV network: Sales through the air with the greatest of ease

PERSONIFICATION

Automatic range: Unties your apron strings

Candy: The sweetheart of a chewsy world (*pun*)

Ketchup: The best pal a good meal ever had

Magazine: Speaks the language of humanity

Tire: The tire that laughs at flats

Girdle: Leaves you breadth-less

Milk: Moo power to you!

Potato chips: Merry Crisp-ness!

Stapler: Does so many fasten-ating things

Station wagon: Tops the tote-em poll

Water softener: America's wash-word

REPETITION

Dress: Makes women look nice and men look twice (*rhyme*)

Drug store: Be safe, be sure, be thrifty—buy Rexall! (*alliteration*)

Noodles: For balanced meals on balanced budgets

REVERSAL

Cancer fund: Check cancer with a cancer check

Paint: Use a good finish, and finish for good

Pen: Exactly right to write exactly

Radio station: People listen to us because we listen to people

Zipper: Smoothly finished to finish smoothly

RHYME

Apple: An apple a day keeps the doctor away

Beverage: More bounce to the ounce

Bus: Convenience plus—go by bus

Carpet: Home means more with carpet on the floor.

Coffee: Toasting protects what blending perfects (*alliteration*)

Magazine: Its best reference is public preference (*alliteration*)

Meat: The ham what am

Paper cup: A better cup from bottom up (*alliteration*)

Pull-out tissues: No fumble—no jumble—no grumble (*triad, repetition*)

Zipper: It hides as it slides

SIMILARITY

Coffee: There's more pick-up per cup

Ice cream: The cheeriest, cherryest ice cream ever

Light bulb: A good buy to see by

Magazine: Spokesman for America's sportsmen

Percolator: Change bitter coffee to better coffee

SPONSOR SLANT

Camera: If it isn't an Eastman, it isn't a Kodak

Cereal: If the last flake crackles—it's Kellogg's

Frozen food: Only the finest is chosen to be frozen by Libby's.

Gasoline: Stop at Sunoco—go with confidence! (*contrast*)

TRIAD

Auto: Eye it—try it—buy it! (*rhyme*)

Beer: Purity, body, flavor

Magazine: Brief, thrilling, authentic

Razor blade: Look sharp—feel sharp—be sharp! (*repetition*)

Shortening: Easy to blend, easier to bake, easiest to digest (*repetition*)

Vacuum cleaner: It beats, as it sweeps, as it cleans (*similarity of "ee" sound*)

Washington State: It's cool, it's green, it's great! (*alliteration*)

WORD PLAY

Awning: Just a shade better

Ballpoint pen: Write on the ball

Bra: Your bosom friend (*personification*)

Lawn sprinkler: Dew it yourself

Savings bank: A weekly habit that grows on you

Shirt: Give your beau an Arrow (*analogy*)

Typical Winning Slogans

To note how some of the foregoing methods were successfully applied in typical contests, consider first the "Slogan for Wood" competition sponsored by the National Lumber Manufacturing Association, which awarded prizes for the following entries:

First, $5,000: Certified by centuries of service (*alliteration*)

Second, $2,000: Wood—use it; nature renews it (*rhyme, balanced phrase*)

Other winning slogans in this contest embodied various techniques as indicated:

Build better with better lumber (*repetition, alliteration*)

For building needs, lumber leads (*rhyme, alliteration*)

110

A growing supply for a growing demand (*repetition, double meaning*)

Your judgment is good when you build with wood (*rhyme*)

The more you use it, the better you like it (*balanced phrase*)

Always in demand—always at hand (*rhyme, repetition*)

Ever growing in forest and in favor (*alliteration, double meaning*)

Wood ways are wise ways (*alliteration, repetition*)

Wood serves, survives and satisfies (*triad, alliteration*)

Another contest, requiring slogans for the Nationwide Trailer Rental System, brought forth these winners, exemplifying methods which should be recognizable by now:

First, $1,000: A little pull goes a long way

Second, $500: The haul of fame

Third, $100: The greatest tow on earth

Other prizes were awarded for these trailer slogans:

Nationwide coast to coast—costs the least, hauls the most

So easy to become attached to us

We lower the high cost of leaving

Moving near, moving far—load a trailer, not your car

Safe-Driving Slogans

Of all slogan themes, the one most often used in contests is safety. This subject, in turn, is divided into two parts—safety in driving and safety elsewhere.

For your guidance in future contests of this nature, consider these three top prizewinners in different safe-driving slogan competitions:

Drive like lightning and you will crash like thunder.

This slogan won a $15,000 car plus $1,000 in cash in a contest conducted by Walter Winchell in behalf of the Damon Runyon Cancer Fund. It is based on analogy—using storm words, "lightning" and "thunder."

Budget your speed after dark—live within your beams.

This won a deluxe sedan in General Motors' contest for a slogan about driving at night. Like the Winchell winner, it is based mainly on analogy, tying in the monetary word "budget" with a parody on another pecuniary expression—"live within your means."

Safety isn't measured by a broken rule.

A new car every year for life was awarded by Dodge for this slogan, which employs double meaning and related words, "measured" and "rule."

Other safe-driving slogans, including some major winners, follow:

Wild dashes from by-ways cause crashes on highways.

Drive so your license expires before you do.

Big mistake many make—rely on horn instead of brake.

Drivers seeking first rights sometimes get their last rites.

Children should be seen and not hurt.

From bar to car to Gates Ajar.

Don't make safety first your last resort.

Hardly a driver is now alive who passed on hills at 75.

Slow down—death begins at 40.

Thinking drivers never drink—drinking drivers never think.

The shortest way to a hospital is through a red light.

Careful drivers are survivors.

Don't hug the car ahead—it's going steady.

Accidents lurk where brakes don't work.

Try saving lives instead of saving time.

Safety pays—speeders pay.

Drivers who think first, last!

Don't take a chance—that chance may take you.

Alert today—alive tomorrow.

If you care to keep working, keep working with care.

Absence of accidents depends upon presence of mind.

Never be haphazard with a fire hazard.

Don't play in fun with a loaded gun.

When crossing streets, use your head and save your neck.

Don't be half safe—look both ways.

Fix carpet rip before you trip.

Play safe and you'll play longer.

Accidents are lamentable—but they're also preventable!

Chapter 12

ANALOGY IN ACTION

After reading all foregoing chapters describing winning techniques, you will have observed that many methods appear repeatedly—having proved successful in every kind of contest cited so far.

While rhyme appears to be the most often used device in winning entries of all varieties, that method has been thoroughly covered in preceding pages and needs no further endorsement.

Analogy, however, which ranks next to rhyme as a specific winning factor, merits more attention than has been given to it before in this book. The author has good reason to acknowledge the importance of analogy because of the many worthwhile awards she has won using this technique. Countless contestants have discovered that this formula, above all others, is simple to employ and helps capture terrific prizes, time and again.

What is Analogy?

Simply defined for prizewinning purposes, analogy is the description of your contest subject in terms borrowed from an entirely different field. For example, here is a 50-word statement that won a vacation for two in Puerto Rico:

It pays to be courteous on subways and buses because . . .
Courtesy is the OIL that smooths the TRACKS of daily
travel, takes the FRICTION out of crowded contacts,
keeps all passengers in pleasant GEAR, and lets the
WHEELS of regular riding roll along with smiling, not
riling, results.

Even a novice contester can see how those emphasized words on travel can be adapted to describe the virtues of almost any other subject or product. Of more direct benefit, though, may be an account of how analogy was employed to make this entry a grand prize winner.

How a Top Prize Was Won

As you will recall from recurrent advice in earlier chapters, compiling lists of appropriate words is an essential preparation for composing suitable entries in virtually every contest that you may try, if the contest involves any form of creative writing.

For this particular Transit Authority contest, on the subject of courtesy in bus and subway, two separate word lists seemed to be required—one dealing with the mechanical or physical features of rapid transit, and the other with mental or emotional attitudes toward such travel. When completed, these two lists contained the following terms:

Transit Words

brake	fast	passenger	stand
bus	friction	platform	station
car	gear	rapid	token
carry	grease	ride	train
conductor	jostle	rider	transport
convenient	lubricate	roll	travel
crowd	motorman	seat	track
fare	oil	shove	wheel

Attitude Words

annoy	decent	manners	right
behave	fair	mutual	rile
bother	fuss	pleasant	rough
consideration	Golden Rule	polite	rude
contact	good will	practice	smile
courteous	harmony	relations	smooth
courtesy	impolite	respect	treat

There are two ways to create analogy entries from such lists. The first method is to utilize analogs that relate directly to your subject. That is what was done in the prizewinning entry in the Transit Authority contest.

115

Mulling over two reference lists, the writer of this entry noticed that "friction" could apply equally well to mechanical action or human relations. How can friction be overcome? In machinery, by some form of lubrication, usually oil. Among crowded passengers, courtesy would be the natural "oil" to reduce annoying friction.

Addition of a few more analogs, such as *tracks, gear,* and *wheels*, with fitting phrases, resulted in construction of the quoted entry, which turned out to be a top prizewinner.

Brainwork, Not Brawnwork, Wins

Revealing the next winning example which utilizes analogy has a two-fold purpose. The first is the excellence of the entry, which illustrates how a good contest writer can employ this fail-proof formula to perfection. The second purpose is as important as the first: Jan Ruehling, the writer of this winning entry, is handicapped. Jan says, "I'm always hesitant to go into details about myself for the simple reason that I like to compete with my fellow contesters on the same level — brainwork, not brawnwork. Contesting was a God-send to me when I first realized that there was more I couldn't do than do; however, brain-wise, I feel on an equal footing, and contesting continues to allow me to express and exercise that!"

Ms. Ruehling's winning combination consisted of a recipe for safe driving employing "recipe" phraseology. Here is her entry:

Batter-not Piece-of-cake Driving

> Pre-heat "thinking" oven.
> Spurn the HALF-BAKED idea that you drive perfectly; therefore, Safe Driving is the "other guy's" responsibility!
> SNAP together Seat Belt, firmly, not GINGERly.
> Put all problems, worries "ON ICE" before starting car; CONCENTRATE PUREly on operating your vehicle properly.
> BLEND SMOOTHLY with the flow of traffic.
> COMBINE Safety Sense and Common Sense in nEGGotiating the roadways.
> GRATE-NOT upon other drivers' nerves by honking your horn unnecesSARA-LEE!
> BEAT-NOT trains to railroad crossings; Stop! Look! and Lessen your chances of getting "CREAMED!"

DASH-NOT down any alcoholic beverages before driving, or you may get DASHED TO BITS!

WHIP-NOT speed beyond lawful limits, or you may have to stop suddenly, and wind up with whiplash!

SALT your driving Lavishly with Courtesy.

PEPPER your driving Well with Patience.

SWEETEN your driving Nicely with Humor.

GARNISH your driving Generously with Alertness.

KNEAD more "Thyme" to reach your destination because of weather conditions?

DOUGHn't LOAF around and leave home later, leave earlier!

Driving safely may not always be a "Piece of Cake," but if you follow this Recipe EGGSactly, you won't end up SCRAMBLED all over the road, or become known as the CRUMB who causes so many accidents!

Categories and Concrete Examples

Analogy classifications are almost endless, and may include terms in any well-known field—art, music, acting, sports (in its manifold branches), financial, naval, military, and scores of others, as illustrated in the following outstanding examples.

Using NAUTICAL picture words to keep her entry AFLOAT in an OCEAN of dull entries, this winner wrote about Coats & Clark's threads or zippers:

I admire OCEANS of colors, desire SEALS of quality, demand Coats efficiency to ANCHOR fabrics flawlessly . . . keeping my SHIP AHOY wardrobe SAILING SMOOTHLY on STARBOARD.

A Lustre-Creme contest called for a last line to the sponsor's given three lines, and here are some winning last lines which demonstrate analogy:

Starting lines:

For shinier, easier-to-manage hair
Try Hollywood's favorite beauty care
It's famous Lustre-Creme Shampoo

Winning lines:

1. INVEST! Let men's INTEREST accrue! (banking)
2. That "GROOMS" him, too, and ALTARS you. (bridal)
3. BUOYS up SUNK curls, FLOATS free true hue. (nautical)
4. This TOP STUNT MAN cuts FILM, "KLIEGS" hue! (Hollywood)
5. REFRESHER COURSE for FLUNKED hairdo. (education)

This statement, which won a Columbia diamond ring, utilizes "labor" terminology:

Everyone should help fight cancer because cancer never STRIKES — indifference, ignorance and neglect keep cancer steadily and contentedly EMPLOYED; only ever-alert ceaseless research can needle cancer into total UN-EMPLOYMENT.

The hunting sport was woven into a statement for a St. Joseph drugstore statement contest, in this manner:

I trade at Leton's Pharmacy because . . . when HUNT-ING savings I get that CENT at Leton's, where HIGH CALIBER products, service that AIMS to please, and friendly atmosphere make me EASY PREY.

In a Krey contest calling for statements telling why you love America, a winner used an orchard analogy to picture the freedom we enjoy:

There is no forbidden FRUIT on its TREE of Freedom; all can PICK PLENTIFULLY, so long as they don't disturb its GROWTH and PRODUCTIVITY.

In a Yamahauler Dodge statement contest, one winner selected this musical analogy:

To my STAFF of six, a YAMAHAULER would bring HARMONY to scout trips, camp-outs, and FUNdamental family affairs; the YAMAHA'S MUSIC TO MY EARS — A SHARP contrast to my Indian that came over on the ark — together A HIT IN TUNE with today.

118

In The National Safety Council's limerick contest, calling for a last line to complete their given four, a clothing analogy was employed in this way:

> Wintertime driving's one test
> Where hazards ahead can't be guessed.
> Think ahead, take it easy
> When roadways are freezy
> SLIPS will show if your tread's MINI-DRESSED.

Planning a Prizeworthy Winner

How do you compose prizeworthy entries such as these? Suppose you had to describe why you prefer to shop at a particular store, which is a perennial contest topic.

If you happen to be a typical consumer, you'd probably think first of "quality with economy" as a good reason for dealing anywhere. But that in itself is too trite and obvious as the basis for a contest entry. So you think a little deeper along that line—how can you prove you're getting quality merchandise at thrifty prices? How? By checking values with similar offers in other stores.

Now the word "checking" stirs a new thought in your mind. Recognizing it as a term used in chess, you look up your lists of game analogs. Under "chess and checkers" you may find all these related words:

advance	checkers	enemy	lose
advantage	checkmate	exchange	man
attack	chess	expert	maneuver
beat	chessman	file	master
beginner	color	force	mate
bishop	concentrate	forward	menace
block	corner	gambit	mobility
blunder	counter	game	movable
board	crown	give up	move
capture	defeat	guard	objective
caution	defend	hostile	offense
castle	defense	interpose	opponent
challenge	development	jump	opposition
champion	diagonal	king	parry
check	draw	knight	partner

pastime	protect	sacrifice	threat
patience	queen	score	tie
pawn	rank	skill	tournament
penalty	remove	square	trap
piece	resign	stalemate	victor
play	retreat	strategy	win
position	rook	tactics	withdraw
problem	row	take	yield

Rewarding Results

Choosing judiciously from this wealth of material, you can soon create an unusual and outstanding entry of winning caliber, incorporating several chess analogs, like this:

> I prefer to shop at Food Fair because . . . by CHECKING values, I've found my smartest MOVE was to Food Fair, always on the SQUARE and above BOARD, pleasing me and my MATE.

This entry and collection of chess terms first appeared in *Contest Magazine* (a magazine now extinct due to the retirement of its editor, Hugh Freese) as part of a series called "Analogy Anthology."

Analogy Anthology Available

Due to popular demand, when the series ended, *Analogy Anthology* was published in paperback by A. D. Freese and Sons, Inc., the publishers of the now out-of-print Contest Magazine. *Analogy Anthology*, in book form, consists of 65 groups of related subjects in alphabetical order ("academic" to "zodiac" analogs) for use in creating sparkling analogies for many types of contests as well as in various other forms of writing. (See examples cited by famous writers and columnists in the preface to this volume.)

Since analogy is such a useful and valuable tool for all forms of writing, *Analogy Anthology* is now in its third printing. It is available for $4.59, while supplies last, from:

> Selma B. Glasser
> 241 Dahill Road
> Brooklyn, NY 11218

The samples cited in this chapter are intended only to whet your writing appetite and aptitude, and spur your own creative power and ingenuity. Analogy provides the steppingstones, but you must pave your own pathway to prizes using this formula.

Chapter 13

SOURCES OF SUCCESS

This volume is intended to cover every major field of creative writing for commercial contests, short fillers, and sweepstake contests, as comprehensively as necessary for your complete information.

However, there is one vital element of this engrossing hobby which obviously cannot be included in any book. That phase would involve providing details of all new contests as they are announced, with specific assistance for each one of importance.

Only magazines or news bulletins, published regularly, can render such specialized, up-to-the-minute service for contestants. "How-To" courses serve as invaluable aids, also.

Of course, you may encounter occasional ads announcing new contests through your favorite daily paper, general magazine, radio, or TV. But that's a hit-or-miss approach to contesting.

If you really wish to make this a profitable hobby, you'll want to keep abreast of all worthwhile prize offers that appear at frequent intervals in many varied media.

Profitable Periodicals and Home Study Courses

To accomplish that purpose, you should get acquainted with some or all of the contest periodicals and home study courses to be described in this chapter. After becoming familiar with the kind of help and information that they provide, you can then decide which of them would be likely to benefit you most as a subscriber.

The following publications are recommended:

EGGLESTON ENTERPRIZE

Eggleston Enterprize, dealers in boxtops, labels, wrappers, and entry blanks for the contest-wise, publishes at irregular intervals depending on the volume of contests during a certain period of time (usually a month or so). This bulletin provides inestimable assistance to serious hobbyists. It announces news of current contests, and offers for sale boxtops, entry forms, and other related items which may be difficult to obtain.

Niles Eggleston started the *Circular Service Contest Bulletin* (CSCB) in the early 1940s. During the depression days of the 1930s, Niles was an active and successful contestant. He started swapping those elusive qualifiers (boxtops, labels, and entry blanks) with fellow hobbyists. This led to his current bulletin, which not only lists the requirements for the latest contests and sweepstakes, but also sells those hard-to-find, but necessary, contest prerequisites for a moderate fee.

In 1960, Niles Eggleston wrote a book entitled *How to Change Boxtops into Dollars,* which is out of print at present. (It has appeared in Braille, also.) His slogan tells it like it is: "Eggleston can help you ENTER and win a PRIZE." A sample copy may be obtained for 65¢, 12 issues for $6.50, from EGGLESTON ENTER-PRIZE, 21 Main Street, Milford, NY 13807.

GLASSER GUIDE

Glasser Guide to Filler Writing is a home-study mail-order course created by the author of this book. An experienced and accomplished prizewinner and filler writer, she teaches a course at Brooklyn College entitled: "Writing for Prize and Publication." Her biographical data is included in *Who's Who of American Women, World's Who's Who of Women* (Cambridge, England), and other prestigious publications. Ms. Glasser's "how-to" articles on writing have been featured in *The Writer* and *Writer's Digest*. Her monthly columns appear in *Golden Chances* and *Prizewinner*. Her fillers and articles may be found in most of the major magazines and newspapers, from time to time. Prizes in contests come her way frequently.

In 1979, Ms. Glasser served as Early Bird chairperson for the National Contesters' Association's 40th Anniversary convention in Philadelphia. She also conducts writing seminars and acts as workshop leader at the annual Philadelphia Writers' Conference.

Her experience and background make *Glasser Guide to Filler Writing* a unique and one-of-a-kind home-study course. There is no other contest or writing course that is personally written by someone who is actually writing and selling the material which the lessons are all about. As Selma Glasser states: "I PRACTICE WHAT I TEACH!"

The course is a roundup of news, views, tips, and techniques on how to win prize contests, and how to create and sell short fillers. As a published writer and award winner, she shares her original work, writing experiences, samples and examples for easy, practical reference and home-study. *GLASSER GUIDE TO FILLER WRITING* is sold on a complete 10-day, money-back guarantee of satisfaction or refund. It covers everything from prize pursuing, greeting cards, comedy basics (THE JOAN RIVERS STORY), puns and parodies, to light verse. It includes pertinent publishing information plus a comprehensive and thoroughly researched list of the major filler markets, syndicates, and greeting card companies—their requirements and rate of pay.

For free information on this 15-lesson home-study course, send a self-addressed, stamped envelope to:

> Selma B. Glasser
> 241 Dahill Road,
> Brooklyn, NY 11218

GOLDEN CHANCES

Golden Chances, a bulletin "dedicated to better contesting," is a monthly newsletter that lists current contests and sweepstakes. In addition, it features a column called "Write-On" written by the author of this volume. This column usually offers thoroughly researched information on how to write for the major magazines and newspapers, and, from time to time, pointers plus winning help on current creative contests.

The publisher of this bulletin, Tom Lindell, tells us that he won his first contest prize when he was seven years of age. He has been hooked on the hobby ever since. In 1974, Tom Lindell's *Golden Chances* was born.

Although single copies sell for $1, a free issue may be obtained by mentioning this book. Twelve issues sell for $10, and a two-year subscription costs $18. Enclose a self-addressed stamped envelope, and write to:

> Tom Lindell's *Golden Chances*, Dept. B
> P.O. Box 655,
> South Pasadena, CA 91030

Prizewinner, Post Office Box 10596, St. Petersburg, FL 33733, and/or 2901–28th Street North (same city and zip) is published monthly by Robert Spence Publications, Inc., and billed as "The World's Leading Contest Magazine." Edward L. Lee is editor. This magazine specializes in puzzle contests, but also includes columns from prominent writers on current creative and sweepstake contests. It features a monthly cash cartoon captioning competition, "Laughable Legends." A column on literary and competitive writing contests entitled, *"$50 an Idea, Why Not?"*, by Selma Glasser, is featured monthly. Single copies sell for $1 and the subscription rate is $10 per year.

SHEPHERD CONFIDENTIAL CONTEST BULLETIN

Issued once a month, this bulletin is owned by Howard E. Doerr, and published by the Shepherd School, Post Office Box 366, Willingboro, NJ 08046.

This school, known in full as the Shepherd Correspondence School of Contest Technique, was founded in 1931 by Wilmer S. Shepherd, Jr., who is responsible for the winning lessons and special features that make his course and bulletin so popular and effective.

Mr. Shepherd is famous in the contest field for imbuing his students with the spirit and knowledge that have made so many of them notably successful in capturing major prizes. His exceptional talent for conveying the ability to win is manifest in every issue of the *Shepherd Confidential Contest Bulletin*.

Its slogan, "Shears for the Golden Fleece," graphically and accurately describes the aims and accomplishments of the *Shepherd Bulletin*, as attested by the great number of winning entries published therein.

Anyone may subscribe to the bulletin. The subscription rate is $9.50 per year (12 issues). A sample issue may be secured upon request at the cost of $1.00.

The Shepherd Coaching Course in Contest Winning is available at the cost of $40, if payment is made in full at the time of enrollment, or $48 on the installment plan.

Of all the publications described here, you will note that only two are home-study courses, namely, *Glasser Guide to Filler Writing* and *The Shepherd School.* The others mentioned are monthly magazines or bulletins which can be subscribed to on a yearly basis or at the single-issue price listed. The latter periodicals keep one abreast of current doings in the contest field on an up-to-the-minute basis, while the former courses illustrate, inspire and instruct in the various writing and prizewinning techniques required for successful creative pursuits.

Literary Sources of Success

If your creative interest in contests includes literary as well as commercial prize offers, either of these major writers' magazines will serve to keep you well informed on markets and instructions:

The Writer, 8 Arlington Street, Boston, MA 02116. Single copies are $1; subscription rate is $12 per year. There is a special rate for new subscribers and students which might be worth investigating. Once a year, *The Writer* publishes *The Writer's Handbook,* which, in addition to listing thousands of markets, includes articles by authors of renown, such as Paul Gallico, Judith Guest, and Joyce Carol Oates. The author of this volume is included in this annual edition.

Another book well worth mentioning, also put out by the editors of *The Writer*, is entitled *How to Write and Sell Fillers, Light Verse and Short Humor*, and costs $7.95. This volume includes 12 chapters by experienced editors and authors—Richard Armour, Mary T. Dillon, Selma Glasser, and others who share some "how-tos" and "where-tos" to help both the beginner and the established writer. Tips on light verse, short humor, epigrams, contests, and all sorts of short fillers are included along with 200 markets showing where to sell, what the editors want, payment rates, how to submit, etc. *How to Write an Sell Fillers, Light Verse, and Short Humor* combines entertaining reading (articles by top authors) with sound instruction, and offers examples that are as amusing as they are helpful.

Writer's Digest, 9933 Alliance Road, Cincinnati, OH 45242, single issues $1.25; subscription rate, $15 per year. This magazine has an annual contest for best articles, short stories, and poetry entries with substantial prizes awarded. The contest is usually announced in the January to June issues. They publish *Writer's Markets* annually, which sells for $14.95. It features thousands of markets for your articles, novels, short stories, plays, etc., also tips on how to submit your work, how much to charge, etc.

A smaller how-to magazine, put out once a year, by *Writer's Digest*, also, is *The Writer's Yearbook*, which costs about $2.95. This paperback contains tips on writing for various markets with hundreds of top markets for fiction, nonfiction, poetry, and books.

Tools of the Trade

If contest periodicals may be considered "Sources of Success"— as indeed they are—then equally worthy of mention in this category are the other implements needed by contesters to pursue their hobby in the most efficent manner possible. Such "tools of the trade" should include some or all of the following books (besides this one and *Analogy Anthology* of course)!

> The latest edition of any standard dictionary—preferably an abridged version that is comprehensive but not too cumbersome for ready reference.
> A thesaurus of synonyms and antonyms. An excellent modern edition of *Roget's Thesaurus* is available in pocket size.
> A rhyming dictionary. Books of this type by Burgess Johnson, Langford Reed, and Clement Wood are much alike in scope and arrangement, and equally valuable for convenient consultation. The Walker-Dawson edition is designed differently, not quite as easy to use, but with word definitions as well as rhymes.

While these rhyming dictionaries are large, cumbersome, and costly, there is a very inexpensive 8½" by 11" simple rhyming dictionary available from the author of this book. It packs easily and contains most of the popular rhymes necessary for short filler writing, limericks, and verse. It costs $3 (plus 59¢ postage).

> A volume of quotations, proverbs, and familiar sayings.
> A book of famous poems, and another of nursery rhymes (for style and parody).

Compilations of jokes, anecdotes, and humorous verse.

Collections of popular limericks, such as those edited by
Bennett Cerf and Louis Untermeyer.

While most books of this kind are available for borrowing or reference at public libraries, you will find it much more convenient to possess your own copies for handy consultation at home. Properly utilized, they can help you win prizes that will soon repay their cost—plus plenty of profit.

Such volumes are obtainable through local book dealers.

More Tools for Mining Contest Gold

In addition to helpful books and magazines, what other equipment should you have in your Winning Workshop? Not everything that follows is essential; but all are desirable items.

You should keep on hand a supply of good-quality writing paper, for entries that are not required to be submitted on official blanks. Envelopes should be large enough to take your entries without folding more than twice. Index cards, 3 × 5 inches in size, are quite suitable for short entries and sweepstakes, and fit into even small envelopes.

Plain white cards or paper can make attractive entries if properly prepared; but if you prefer to use lightly tinted stationery, no contest judge is likely to object to it.

Clear-writing, non-smudging pens in various colors should be available for appropriate usage; but your signature should always be in discreet blue or black ink.

A small loose-leaf notebook, which can be carried around handily, will serve well for recording stray thoughts on current contests, as they occur to you. Such random ideas can later be worked into full-fledged entries, when you have access to your complete file of reference material.

An asset to any contester is a typewriter, preferably an electric one. This book was typed with a Smith-Corona "Vantage" with changeable typing elements (for variety). Its ribbon cassettes make it a snap to change. It made the job a lot easier.

However, while typewritten entries may be favored for legibility by some contest judges, it is *not* necessary to type your entries in order to win—unless the rules so specify. Thousands of contestants have won major prizes with entries that were *neatly* and *clearly* printed or written by hand.

Filing for the Future

Aside from its legibility, a typewriter has one important advantage for contestants over handwriting—it makes better carbon copies, for more convenient filing. The "Vantage" mentioned earlier makes excellent photostats.

If you are completely new to the contest hobby, you may wonder why it is advisable to make and keep copies of your entries. The best answer is simply—reference value. By saving all past entries, you will gradually accumulate a rich storehouse of your own material that may be reworked, refined, and reused in future contests, whether or not such entries won before.

Another good reason for keeping copies of your entries is to compare them with published winners in the same contests, to see what improvements may be needed in efforts that may have failed to win. Such comparisons can often prove exceedingly helpful in showing you what it takes to capture a prize.

For filing copies of your own entries, as well as contest ads, bulletins, and other pertinent data, you should use manila file folders, available at any stationery store. At the start of your contesting career, a table or desk drawer may be sufficient to store this material; but eventually you will want a regular filing cabinet—which can be paid for out of your winnings in due time.

Twelve Typical Toppers

So far, this chapter has covered such sources of success in contesting as books, magazines, and other "tools of the trade"—all valuable, all important, but all inanimate.

To many contesters, though, the most inspiring wellspring of success is the positive knowledge that other people like themselves have achieved fame and fortune in the same field of endeavor.

"What they can do, I can do!" That enthusiastic emotion is the magic key that unlocks the door of doubt and lets you enter the vault of victory. And what could be more evocative of such enthusiasm than to learn what other people have won, who they are, and where they live? Listed here are just a few noteworthy winners—an even dozen selected from various parts of the country—whose prize attainments may well encourage you to keep trying until similar success comes your way.

ALABAMA: Mrs. Lillou McCain of Birmingham won two cars from General Mills and $5,000 from Procter & Gamble, among other prizes.

CALIFORNIA: Mrs. Nita Parks of Pasadena has won more than $40,000 in prizes, including one of $25,000 for a last line in a Colgate jingle contest.

COLORADO: Mrs. Sybil Todd of Denver won two overseas vacation trips within a single year, one to Europe and the other to the Orient.

FLORIDA: Mrs. Nancy Ungaro of North Miami won $30,000 for a statement about a Zenith television set.

MINNESOTA: Mrs. Deborah Schneider of Minneapolis won $500 a month for life for 25 words about Plymouth cars.

MISSOURI: Mrs. Grace Ellen Tousley of Independence won her weight in gold—amounting to exactly $50,318.06—for a statement about the Easy Combomatic Washer-Dryer.

NORTH CAROLINA: Stanford Mizelle of Raleigh won $25,000 in a Colgate picture title contest.

OHIO: Albert M. Husted of Cincinnati won three automobiles in less than one year in statement and slogan contests.

OKLAHOMA: Dale Kelley of Oklahoma City won a month's vacation with his family at a chateau on the French Riviera in Gulf Oil's jingle contest.

OREGON: Mrs. Dorette Lemon of Portland won free food for life (at the rate of $25 worth a week) in a Betty Crocker–Sunkist contest for naming a pie "Lemon Dorette"— a transposition of her own name!

TEXAS: Donald Parkinson of Dallas, grand prize winner in a Dial Soap jingle contest, was given his choice of $25,000 cash or the income from an active oil well. He took the cash award.

WASHINGTON: George Hill of Seattle won more than 3,794 separate prizes in his long contest career.

Comradeship in Contesting

To read about these contest stars and their amazing accomplishments is indeed thrilling to prize seekers who aspire to similar goals. Even more thrilling to many contest fans would be a chance to meet some famous winners in person, talk to them, and hear them relate their own success stories. If such encounters appeal to you, by all means join the National Contesters Association, where comradeship in the keynote.

This organization, whose aim is to have "Every member a winner and every winner a member," was founded in 1937 by Everett Lane, of Fredericksburg, VA. Since then, NCA (as the association is known in the contest field) has held annual conventions in different cities throughout the nation.

NCA conventions are attended by several hundred enthusiastic prize pursuers every year, eager to hear words of wisdom from outstanding winners, teachers, editors, judges, sponsors, advertising specialists, and other people prominent in the contest world.

Recent conventions have been held in Philadelphia, PA (where the author of this book recently acted as "early bird" chairperson), Buffalo, NY; Boston, MA; Miami Beach, FL; Denver, CO; San Antonio, TX and in various other parts of the country.

In addition to the sociability and mutual assistance it offers all members, NCA has a particularly worthy purpose—to bring the benefits of the contest hobby to shut-in or handicapped people, including hospitalized war veterans. To such "Winsiders," as NCA calls them, this engrossing pastime offers not only monetary but therapeutic rewards.

NCA dues are $6 annually. This organization publishes a bimonthly bulletin. A contestant need not attend annual conventions to become a member and receive news of activities relating to NCA. Since NCA officers change annually, additional details and the latest free information about NCA may always be obtained by writing:

> NCA
> % Selma B. Glasser
> 241 Dahill Road
> Brooklyn, NY 11218

A self-addressed stamped envelope or return postage should always be enclosed when requesting a reply.

While NCA is the only nationwide organization for contest fans, there are several regional associations of prize seekers, which conduct their own conventions. Many cities have contest clubs that hold monthly meetings, where newcomers to this hobby are as welcome as regular winners.

So, you see, there are many sources of success in the wondrous world of contesting—books, magazines, courses, societies—with inspiration for individual achievement to be found in all of them.

Chapter 14

PATTERNS FOR PROFIT

Long-experienced prizewinners, who have followed the contest hobby for many years, can skip this little chapter without missing anything not already known to them.

However, for newcomers to what has been aptly called "the pastime that pays," the subject briefly treated here should prove both revealing and rewarding. It will cover certain well-known winning ways, not previously mentioned because of their rather limited effectiveness.

These patterns, formulas or entry designs—as they are variously termed—have been used by knowing contestants in countless competitions with consistent success. In fact, such forms have been employed so many times that some of them have become recognizable from repetition, and can no longer capture major prizes in national contests.

Limited to Locals

Nevertheless, winning entries published in the very latest contest bulletins demonstrate beyond a doubt that even the most familiar versions of patterned entries still continue to win regularly in local contests—and occasionally in those of broader scope.

Perhaps there is more prestige in winning a national contest prize than a local award. But, as Gertrude Stein might have said, a car is a car is a car—and a brand new Cadillac presented to you by a neighborhood merchant in a community contest is worth just as much as if you had won it in a highly publicized nationwide competition sponsored by General Motors itself. And, of course, a thousand dollars in cash is a "grand" award—no matter who gives it to you.

So whenever you are tempted to try a contest confined to your own home town or shopping area, the following formulas will facilitate your entry writing—especially in composing short statements—for they help to organize your thoughts along certain lines that seem to find perennial favor with judges of locally limited prize offers.

When rules of such community contests allow you to submit more than a single entry in the same competition, it would be generally advisable to include your choice of some of these potentially profitable patterns, since you never can tell when your "pick" may strike gold!

Admire-Desire-Require Form

(This is the grandpa of all prize patterns—but there's life in the old boy yet!)

> My favorite store features styles I *admire*, products I *desire,* and bargains I *require*.

> This paint provides the finish I *admire*, the surface I *desire*, and the durability I *require*.

Alphabet Form

> Filled with healthful vitamins, this food gives me a "B"-eneficial meal with "D"-elightful taste and "G"-enerous supply of "E"-nergy.

> To men who mind their tobacco P's and Q's, this cigar makes smoking satisfaction as simple as A, B, C.

> I've found them best by every test from "A"-roma clear to "Z"-est.

Arithmetic Form

> This shoe polish *adds* new appearance, *subtracts* scuff marks, and *multiplies* life of footwear.

133

This shortening *adds* delicious flavor, *subtracts* greasiness, *divides* food costs, and *multiplies* mealtime pleasure.

Ease and E's Form

This car combines EASE of driving with the E's of Efficiency, Economy, and Excellence—satisfying Everyone.

Extra Form

This cigaret is *extra* long, *extra* mild, *extra* cool—at no *extra* cost.

Five Senses Form

I can *see* this bread's purity; *feel* its fine texture; *smell* its wheaty fragrance; *taste* its fresh flavor; and *hear* my family praise it.

Healthy-Wealthy-Wise Form

I can be *healthy* with this soda's purity, *wealthy* saving on its quantity, and *wise* in choosing such delicious refreshment.

I'm mouth *healthy* and tooth *wealthy* because I'm *wise* enough to use this dentifrice.

Kind Form

This cigar is *kind* to my throat; *kind* to my tongue; and *kind* to my wallet—therefore, it's my *kind* of smoke.

Password Form

This syrup is the *password* to eager appetites; the *watchword* for wholesome energy; the *buy-word* for economy; and the *last word* for flavor.

This store is the *password* to variety; the *watchword* for reliability; the *buy-word* for bargains; and the *last word* in obliging service.

Pledge of Allegiance Form

This beverage pledges allegiance to good taste and to the purity with which it's made—one flavor individual with energizing effect upon all.

Satisfy Both Form

When my pride demands Class, and my bankbook demands Thrift, I *satisfy both* with this elegant yet inexpensive car.

When hunger urges me to dine out, and my wallet warns me to wait, I *satisfy both* at this popular-priced restaurant.

Singular Form

It's truly a *singular* candy—*one* quality: the highest—*one* flavor: the tastiest—and *one* price: the thriftiest!

A Word to the Wise

When using any of the patterns shown in this chapter, you must remember that they are already familiar to many contestants—and will become known to many more through their publication here.

So, while you may feel free to follow whatever designs you prefer, do not copy any quoted example word for word. Instead, try to originate your own apt expressions to fit the given framework.

Thereby, you can turn entries that were trite into entries that are bright—the kind judges take a shine to every time!

Chapter 15

TOP WINNING ENTRIES

As pointed out in previous chapters, you need no inborn talent to win commercial contests. The contest art can be acquired with training and application. You can learn the basic forms of popular contest writing by reviewing the many contest techniques covered in this book. The countless samples and examples should be studied regularly. They serve as idea starters only, and are not to be copied.

Practice Makes Prizes

Even if you have never written a single entry before, you now have a good grounding in usable variations to activate your own brain power. With a little practice, perseverance, and patience, it will be relatively simple for you to compose write-in entries and receive ample awards.

Hundreds of Winners Revealed

Having access to prize written words is the best education for newcomers as well as old-time contestants, which is the reason this book is so heavily spiced with top winning entries in almost every chapter. Chapter 4 contains 39 winning entries; Chapter 5, 29; Chapter 6, 59; Chapter 7, 61; Chapter 8, 28; Chapter 9, almost 100 winning ones (including entries that won $25,000, $20,000, $10,000 and $5,000); Chapter 10, 57 winners; Chapter 11, over 100 (including entries that won $15,000, $5,000, $2,000 and $1,000 in cash); Chapter 12 includes 14 prize-winning entries and, finally, Chapter 14 about 19 winners.

To further aid you in your continuing quest for contest prizes, this chapter features outstanding top winning entries for comprehensive analysis and study.

Home Winners

This entry won a Grand Prize Celotex Home in the Runyon Cancer Fund Contest, some years back:

Arrest Cancer — It's Wanted for Murder!

An Arizona retirement community was to be named. The prize was a two-bedroom home, for this entry:

Sun City

Large Cash or Merchandise Winning Entries

This one won $12,000 in cash in a Colorado Cancer Control slogan contest:

Make Cancer Control Colorado's Goal

Prizes such as two cars, two refrigerators, a color TV, a record player, bone china, a mink, etc., amounting to $20,000, were given for this name for a hot dog roll:

Bunderful

A plane was awarded for its name which was:

Spin-up girl

Liquore Di Noche needed a name for a drink which called for 2/3 Liquore Di Noche (a walnut-flavored liqueur) and 1/3 sweet cream, on the rocks. Here is the $5,000 grand prize winning name:

Sweet Wally Walnut

In the Safeguard Soap contest sponsored by Proctor & Gamble, contestants were asked to make up a word describing the soap and then write 50 words or less about it. A $5,000 top prize winner wrote:

> Tubmarine — Armed with Triclocarban, Safeguard annihilates foreign body odors that "Run Silent, Run Deep," turning my *husband* AWOL (*A*live *W*ith *O*cean-fresh *L*ather). It *launches* me out of blustery moods into relaxed ones while sharing *tub*quarters with a splashy *sub*ordinate whose diaper rash is soothed, smoothed by this mel-

137

low TUBMARINE. (Note clever use of sea and water terms. See Chapter 12 on analogy, or page 24 of *Analogy Anthology*.)

This letter won the grand prize of a $5,000 U.S. savings bond and an all-expense-paid 7-day vacation for up to four people in Washington, D.C., in the Allerest and Sinarest "Dear Mr. President" statement contest for expressing ideas about our great country in 100 words or less:

> Dear Mr. President:
> Let's face it! The economy is failing and Americans are ready for drastic action now. *Americans have spirit.* Ask us . . . you will find us ready to do more. We will sacrifice, share the burden and readjust our living standards. People will accept compulsory controls and constructive change.
> America cannot afford hesitant halfhearted government. *It is time.* Time to pass a gasoline tax, use an allocation plan, eliminate oil depletion allowances and enact a new tax on oil companies windfall profits.
> We must share the burden. Let's *work together* to rekindle the "Spirit of 76" and revitalize life in America.

This entry won a $5,000 college scholarship by completing this statement:

The Lettermen are today's number one college recording group because . . .

> They are: *A*ccomplished/*B*rilliant/*C*ool/*D*ynamic/*E*ntertaining/*F*UNtastic/*G*o-goinest/*H*ep/*I*nstrumentalented/*J*umping/*K*een/*L*ETTER-perfect/*M*elodelightful/*N*OTEable/*O*utstanding/*P*LAYful/*Q*ualified/*R*hythmic/*S*INGular/*T*UNEtalizing/*U*nBEATable/*V*ocallossal/*W*INsome/*X*citing/*Y*outhful/*Z*esty.

A $5,000 name for Congoleum-Nairn's Vinyl cushionfloor pattern:

Serenity

The $1,000 winners in the same competition entered these names:

Pianissimo — Splendora — Nevamar — Avant Garde — Parader

To name a three-layer dessert, California Donnelley selected this name as a $2,500 prize winner:

Gay Capalayero

Nesbitt's "Orange Man" naming contest awarded first Grand Prize of $2,000 plus the *Encyclopaedia Britannica* for this name:

Squeezix

If you've seen the Soft & Dri commercials which start with "Nervous is . . . ," that's what this contest was all about. The entrant was to write a typical commercial for the product. Grand prize was $3,000 plus an all-expense trip to Hollywood to appear in a Soft & Dri commercial, plus luxurious accommodations in Beverly Hills, private chauffeur-driven limousine, and lots of other extras. The first prize consisted of expensive stereos. The Grand Prize winner wrote:

Nervous is kicking left in the chorus line . . . and everyone else is kicking right.

The First Prize winner wrote:

Nervous is getting your first parakeet . . . the same day your brother brings home a stray cat.

A $2,000 Head Start in Life insurance policy was awarded for a statement of "your chosen career in twenty-five words or less." The winner wrote:

I think a career as a Children's Author is important because a talented writer can widen a child's horizons, teach him awareness of beauty and acceptance of tragedy.

The Knudsen/Diet Delight Salad limerick contest awarded $1,000 for a last line to the sponsor's given four, as follows:
The sponsor's lines:

There's a beautiful salad I'm told
Worth more than its weight in pure gold.
You can make it with ease,
With our peaches and cottage cheese.

The winning completion:

Draw *interest* as weight is controlled.

(Note again the use of analogy, this time DRAW — INTEREST.)

WMCA RADIO wanted a slogan using their call letters, and gave
$1,000 for this winning one:

*W*hy *M*illions *C*hoose *A*udio

A St. Petersburg woman won $1,000 for her money-saving idea:

How my friends and neighbors can whip inflation is by
voting for legislators who do not raise their own salaries,
who do cut fat off pork barrels, and keep in touch with
the ordinary nephews and nieces of an Uncle Sam who
needs to slim down, shape up and watch his morals and
their morale.

The SnoBoy Monkey naming contest went "ape" for this $1,000
winner:

Count Fleas

A first prize of $500 in the Microtone Company's contest to name
a hearing aid went to:

Conversation peace

Huge Jackpot Winner

Top winner of $33,000 for National Kids Day slogan contest went
to this one:

Child by child, we build our nation.

Trip Winning Entries

Peter Heering sponsored a Valentine poetry contest and offered
as prizes three trips for two to Denmark plus $1,000 spending
money (or a cash equivalent for each winner of over $3,500). Here
are the three completions to the following given jingle that won
those prizes:

The sponsor's lines:

> I think of you throughout the day,
> In everything I do and say.
> You are the one I hold most dear,

The winners:

> 1. *My world's become a YOU-shaped sphere.*
> 2. *In "Bank of Love" you're my cashier.*
> 3. *My "Black Book" tossed, let's churchward steer.*

Stella D'Oro awarded a trip to Europe for this entry:

> Stella D'Oro Products are like a tour of the Continent because when HUNGARY there is NORWAY better than to RUSSIAN buy these SWEDEN tasty morsels, crisp as ALPINE air, exciting as PARIS — the flavor ISRAELI delicious.

Datsun Cars awarded a first prize jet trip for two to Japan for this well-worded winning entry:

> I like the new Datsun because it's excitingly redesigned for "years-to-come" smartness, comfort and convenience; economical to run, service and repair, Datsun has smooth oriental beauty with solid occidental practicality.

This rhymed statement won a grand prize of a vacation for two to Rome plus a cash bonus, for telling why the contestant wanted the trip:

> I need a vacation because . . .
> Whether Around the World in 80 days
> Or whirled around in 80 ways,
> With dishes, diapers, dilemmas chronic
> We harried parents need a Roamspun tonic!

A seven-day, six-night trip for two to Palm Springs, California, to attend the Bob Hope Desert Golf Classic with round-trip transportation, accommodations at a first-class luxury hotel plus $75 per day spending money, in the Desenex and Cruex contest, was awarded for 100 words or less on "Why I'd like to win a trip to the Bob Hope Desert Golf Classic at Palm Springs." The winner:

I'M not TEEsing when I say
A housewife's COURSE is no FAIR-WAY;
With pots and pan I daily spar—
My handicap's well over par.
I sweep and mop—I iron and bake,
A DESERT trip, I'd like to take;
I HOPE I gain that CLASSIC glee—
I want to see STARS in person
Not just on TV!

The American Hotel & Motel Association, in an effort to discourage people who make reservations and neglect to cancel when they are unable to come, ran a contest for a slogan. Out of 47,153 entries received, they selected several and awarded valuable trip prizes for each of the following winners:

1. We make reservations about people who fail to keep theirs.
2. Ease the squeeze, and call us please.
3. We'd like to know, if you can't show.
4. Be nice. Think twice. If you can't show, let us know
5. Be a good Scout — call IN to cancel OUT.

This slogan won a dream vacation for two on the Riviera plus $500 in cash from Hollywood Bread:

HOLLYWOOD BREAD—for that weight-less feeling.

A Florida woman described in clever rhyme what her wardrobe would be like if she won a Burdine's cruise:

My sunshine fashion cruise wardrobe on a Grace Line cruise visiting Curacao, La Guaira, Aruba, Kingston, Jamaica, Port-au-Prince, Haiti, would be:

Flats, slippers, pumps and sneakers; socks for tramping streets;
Some kookie combinations; and "little nothing" neats;
Three swim suits, dripless, zipless; in solid solids, natch;
Terry robe for bath and beach; terry scuffs to match;
Snaky ciggy holder; sun spectacles to see;
Blouses, T shirts, muumuus; quick-dry lingerie;
Strapless bra, and girdle; white cotton gloves, cord suit;

Hat for church, cosmetics; pearls, earrings, bumbershoot;
One tremendous straw bag; evening bag, belts, hose;
Slim skirts, full, Jamaicas, slacks; and perfume-for "his"
    nose
Elegant evening sweaters; cocktail dresses, too;
One light coat, a tooth brush—most of this in blue!

The top winning entry in Mifflin Rubbing Alcohol's "Vacation in Spain" contest was:

Shakespeare cried: "Ay, there's the rub!
Mifflin alongside my tub!"
Said Ann, "That's not silly.
It hath-a-way, Willie.
Use Mifflin (with Dermium)—No sub!"

Mink Winner

The winner of the first prize (a $7,500 mink coat) in Jovan's Mink & Pearls contest wrote:

I ... LOVE my neighbor—turn other cheek
Limit "white lies" to one a week!
KILL NOTHING ... except time,
Never WITNESS FALSEly, or commit crime;

Honor my parents—to hubby true—
KEEP THE SABBATH HOLY ... 'fraid not to!
I'm one of the "better girls"
But I COVET ... Mink & Pearls!

Automobile Winners

The winner of an automobile submitted this safety slogan:
Watch your hurry!

A Ford car winner in a St. Louis Hill-Behan Stores contest wrote:

143

Hill-Behan Stores are neighbor-handy
Convenient parking space is dandy,
Modest prices — modern styles,
Change shopping miles to shopping smiles.

Diamond Winner

For a $1,500 Keepsake Diamond Ring in the *Fair Lady Magazine* statement contest, this winner wrote in excellent rhyme:

I like FAIR LADY MAGAZINE because . . .
Beauty — hair — and horoscope,
  My head is in a whirl;
Fiction-fare — and movie-males
  (I'm glad that I'm a girl!)

TV Winner

A Long Island woman won an RCA Home Entertainment Center by writing why she preferred Maremont guaranteed automotive parts for her car, in this jingle:

This Miss never understood
What went 'neath her RIDING-HOOD,
But Maremont's two-year guarantee
Keeps those *Wear-Wolves* 'way from me!

You Are Next

You have observed "top" winning entries from contests in the past. Now it is up to you to build upon these ideas and come up with your own successful endeavors. Perhaps, in a future issue of this book, you will be lucky and smart enough to see your own prize-winning words listed herein. Good luck!

Chapter 16

HOW TO WIN BYLINES IN MAGAZINES AND NEWSPAPERS

For the reader who desires to go one step beyond contest winning, there are numerous markets for short writings of every description. The payment ranges from pin-money to substantial sums, depending upon the publication.

$50 a Word Is Possible

Playboy pays $50 and up for short pieces accepted in their "After Hours" department and also $50 for "Party Jokes." *Good Housekeeping* pays well for light verse, epigrams, and short humor for their "Light Housekeeping" and back-of-the-book fillers. *Saturday Evening Post* uses all sorts of shorts, humorous anecdotes, and quizzes in their "Post Script" department. *American Legion* in "Parting Shots," *Woman's Day* in "Neighbors," etc.

Reader's Digest pays $300 for anecdotes for "Life in These United States," "Humor in Uniform," "Campus Comedy," and "All in a Day's Work." They also buy short contributions for "Toward More Picturesque Speech," "Laughter, The Best Medicine," "Quotable Quotes," and "Personal Glimpses."

Rotarian uses fillers for its "Stripped Gears" column. *Columbia Journalism Review, Editor & Publisher, The Reader's Digest* and others buy previously published, amusing misprints, signs, and mistakes in news stories or headlines. *Catholic Digest* pays from $10 to $50 for serious as well as amusing fillers. Countless others, too numerous to mention, are eager to buy all sorts of shorts from would-be writers.

Purpose of Fillers

It's easy, it's fun and it's lucrative. These fillers liven up the pages of hundreds of magazines and newspapers and are becoming increasingly important to editors. Originally inserted to fill the end of the column or the bottom of the page spaces, they are now featured parts of many publications.

How to Become a Published Writer

Opportunities for writers in this field are exceptionally attractive, especially for the beginner writer. You don't need a famous name to sell an anecdote, light verse, four-line filler, or joke. Simply supply the editor of the particular publication with the type of filler or short humor he wants, and he will buy from you, even if you've never published a single item before.

Similar to contest writing, fillers require a certain amount of expertise in clever phrases, poetic perfection, and many of the techniques already covered in this book. It's also the kind of writing that can be done at any time and in almost any place. A considerable amount of writing can be done while commuting to work, doing household jobs, or having lunch. There is hardly a time when you cannot collect and storage up ideas for publishable short items. Make mental notes of clever things seen, read, or heard as idea starters.

Timeliness

Timeliness is of the essence. Be tuned in to what's new in the world or in your neighborhood.

The word "dope" creates a distasteful picture in one's mind. In my filler, I called "dope" the kid with the low grades. I called "hang-up" (or lack of it) clothes, and "rock" what we do when a baby's crying in the crib.

When "the pill" was making headlines, I sold *Saturday Evening Post* this short:

> Question: How would you define "the pill?"
> Answer: The greatest labor-saving device.

Newsworthy items

Ecology is a topic of today. I sold Improbable Proverbs to *The American Journal of Nursing,* leading off with:

> Still Water Causes Ecology Problems.

A light verse called "Eek-ology" that I sold to a medical journal went like this:

> I'd surely love to take deep breaths
>   But never dared to
> Since learning of the many ills
>   That man is AIRED to!

When the subject of transplants was fresh on everyone's lips, my timeliness again paid off for me in *Playboy's* "After Hours" column this way:

> A Medium's Place for Holding Seances Is Called: *"The Trance Plant."*

Still toying with the word "transplant," I wrote and sold the following to *Medical World News*:

Vital Organ Recital

> My heart is a-quiver.
> I offer my liver,
> My lungs, or a kidney,
> Go on, you can rid me
> Of parts for transplanting—
> Permission I'm granting!
> But would it be dull, sir,
> To offer an ulcer,
> A disk that is slipping,
> A nose that keeps dripping,
> Ugly veins showing,
> Legs hurting and slowing?
> I offer my used parts,
> My much more abused parts.
> A trade-in would please me,
> You might even freeze me:
> Then change parts a-plenty
> Until I feel twenty!

A Filler for All Seasons

Seasonal timeliness is of the utmost importance for fillers. Needless to say, they have to be submitted about six months ahead of the event. For Christmas, this one was submitted in July:

Question: What would you call an unwed Santa?
Answer: Single Kringle.

Timed for a February issue, this light verse, practically, was an instant sale:

Taking a Licking

Though Abe and George were famous men
And give us holidays again,
Where did it get these well-know champs?
They ended up on postage stamps!

This bit of advice found itself in *Medical World News* in time for the holidays:

Advice to those likely to overindulge in food (over the holidays); Remember to Put the Heart Before the Course.

Occasionally, signs spotted in store windows, billboards, or subways lend themselves to double meanings and can be submitted verbatim for a filler sale. How about this one:

SUGGESTIVE MOTHER'S DAY GIFTS

Or in a florist's shop:

OUR BLOOMERS ARE ALWAYS IN FASHION.

APPLY ANALOGY TECHNIQUE IN EPIGRAMS

A quick scanning of my favorite soft-covered, instant, idea-starter book, *Analogy Anthology* (see Chapter 12), practically pays for itself many times over, each usage. Employing FIRE terminology, this epigram appeared in *Playboy*:

A guy with money "to burn" has a good chance of finding a perfect "match."

From *Family Weekly*:

On music: The man who thinks a pretty girl is like "a melody" is usually "dancing" to her "tune."

Punning on popular words or expressions sometimes starts the grey matter perking. We've all been exposed to the phrase "remedial reading." From those two words, I arrived at a punch line pun, and my light verse practically wrote itself:

What Goes Down Must Come Up

Some gardeners excel in their planting and seeding,
By constantly nurturing, cutting and feeding;
Their lawns clearly show that their work is succeeding.

Though I spend weeks of spading, top soiling and pleading,
My plot's a sad lot, which is surely not leading. . .
I'm thinking of taking REMEDIAL WEEDING!

Many times weather forecasters disturb me with their inaccurate predictions of weather for planned outdoor excursions, and here's what emerged:

Weather Flawcasters

Predicting weather, they're so wrong,
With each and every scoop;

That's why forecasters all belong
To a non-PROPHET group!

Combining Puns—Seasons—Timeliness

Epigrams lend themselves to punning. *The Wall Street Journal* liked my economy note, put thusly:

With the high cost of living these days, it's cheaper by the DOESN'T!

This one, with a combination of ingredients, I sent to Harper's:

When egotists meet, their talk develops into an I for an I.

By incorporating seasonal timeliness with puns, I wrote and sold this:

Home Groan

Can I succeed in gardening?
  No, never, never!
Because this thing of beauty is
  A job forever!

At the present time, light verse, epigrams, short anecdotes, and all sorts of short fillers are selling to more publications than ever before. Editors continue to need fresh sources of supply to keep their pages perky, funny, and easy to read quickly. With a little persistence, practice, and study (see Chapter 13, Sources of Success— *Glasser Guide to Filler Writing*) anyone with an interest in words is well on the way to becoming a successful filler writer.

Reprints of columns from *Golden Chances* (see Chapter 13) on how to hit *Reader's Digest, Saturday Evening Post, Playboy,* etc., which include ample samples and examples, may be obtained by sending a self-addressed, stamped envelope for information, to the author of this book.

Chapter 17

HOW TO WIN IN RECIPE CONTESTS

Recipe contests are another tempting type of contest. Creative contestants with a little inventiveness, enterprise, and cooking ability can enjoy tremendous success in this kind of competition.

Huge Recipe Awards

These outstanding recipe contests are worth special mention:

For over 25 years, the Pillsbury Company has sponsored Bake-Off® contests with top prizes of $25,000 at each event. The 1980 competition had a top prize of $40,000 (with a total of more than $100,000 in prizes). A few recent winners are: Mrs. Esther V. Tomich of San Pedro, California, received $25,000 for her Nutty Graham Picnic Cake in contest 28; Mrs. Luella E. Maki of Ely, Minnesota, won $25,000 for her Sour Cream Apple Squares in contest 26; and Mrs. Barbara S. Gibson of Fort Wayne, Indiana, received $25,000 for her Easy Crescent Danish Rolls in the same competition. In these baking contests, Pillsbury's first male prize winner was Jack Meili of Minneapolis, Minnesota. An Oakland, California, man won best-of-class with a cake in contest 15.

The National Chicken Cooking Contest chose Norma Young as their top winner of $10,000 for her Golden Chicken Nuggets, which combined chicken breasts with Mazola oil. Another top winner of $10,000 was Thomas C. Parvis of Montclair, New Jersey, for his Sunshine Chicken. Parvis was one of seven men among the state champions. Another year, in this same contest, Florence Callaghan was crowned champion in the portable appliance division, and her 16-year old daughter, Jane, was crowned junior champion. Mrs. Callaghan's recipe was called Chicken Breast Sandwich; her daughter's winning entry was Chicken A-Go-Go. Jane won a $1,000 shopping spree plus a wardrobe that she selected. Her mother's prize was a houseful of 17 Sunbeam appliances. As top winners, each also received a three-tier McCormack spice rack filled with 24 different spices plus separately engraved sterling silver Revere bowls by Stieff. Mr. Joel Allard of Texas was named barbecue champion at this same event.

The National Pineapple Cooking Classic Cook-Off held in Hawaii awarded Lentsey Carlson of Lakewood, New York, a $10,000 first-place prize in the salad division.

Everyone Is Eligible

If you observed the winners, they were not necessarily women. Men, women, and children have equal chances to compete and win in recipe contests, unless the rules state otherwise.

Recipe Secrets to Be Revealed

Later on in this chapter, you will discover more about these fortunate winners, and how easy it is to win fabulous prizes in recipe contests. Right now, you may be wondering whether such exciting events can happen to you. They can, indeed, if you learn how to apply the winner's recipe secrets revealed here. You will find scores of recipe-contest ideas that can be absorbed and utilized. There is no better way to learn how to concoct winning recipes than to study successful methods employed by previous prizewinners. In this chapter, they are revealed for ready reference as idea-starters to assist you in your culinary efforts.

First, however, let's survey cooking contestdom as a whole, to get an idea of the size and scope of the current cooking contest scene.

Some Notable Recipe Contests

The National Pineapple Recipe Contest offered 40 prizes, each including a trip for two to Hawaii. The finalist in each of four categories won $10,000 and the best-of-contest winner received an additional $15,000 (making $25,000 in all). There were also four runner-up prizes of $2,500 each.

The National Chicken Cooking Contest offered 51 finalists a trip to the national cook-off headquarters plus $100 cash. The prizes they competed for were $10,000, $4,000, $3,000, $2,000, and $1,000.

Lawry awarded five winning entrants an all-expense-paid trip to Los Angeles and $100 a day to compete in the finals for their

World's Greatest Hamburger Recipe Contest. The top winner received $5,000 for a hamburger recipe; runners-up, $500 each.

The National Beef Cook-Off Contest gave away $1,500, $750, $500, and five $100 prizes.

Country Stand's Fresh Mushroom Recipe Contest had 5,029 prizes including a grand prize of free grocery money for three years ($50 a week) and two second prizes of free grocery money for one year ($50 a week apiece).

Borden Sour Cream awarded fourteen prizes, including a first-prize round trip to Disney World, for the winner and three other finalists.

Baskin-Robbins Ice Cream Show-Off Recipe Contest paid off with a grand prize two-week vacation for two on the Hawaiian islands of Oahu, Maui, and Kawai.

National Earthworm Recipe Contest offers $500 annually for the best recipe using earthworms. Some finalists in this one came up with such interesting recipe titles as Quiche Lorraine Avec de Terre, Worm Fritters, Ver de Terre Scudder Botch (Butter Scotch) Delights, etc.

Needless to say, the big daddy of all recipe contests is the Bake-Off® competition sponsored by The Pillsbury Company. They have been awarding $25,000 grand prizes and many other large cash prizes. In the 1980 competition, top prize was $40,000, with more than $100,000 in other cash awards, as well as merchandise.

Although many new cooking contests arrive on the scene from time to time, we can always depend on such sponsors as National Pineapple, National Chicken, and Pillsbury to repeat their competitions.

What the Experts Say

According to food experts like James Beard, originality plays an important role in the determination of a winner in almost any recipe contest. Beard, one of the foremost culinary authorities in the United States, says originality is important, but not just for its own sake. "The recipe must be sound," he says. He further finds that often the wrong cooking utensil is recommended, the cooking time is not accurate, one of the steps is left out, or something is incorrectly identified. "Finally," says Beard, "we take into consideration appearance, smell, texture and taste. Last year, the Seagram's V.O. contest was open in five categories—hors d'oeuvre, soup, salad, entree, and dessert—and I have been asked how one can compare them. What one compares, of course, are the degrees of excellence using the criteria we have discussed."

Robert Jay Misch, a syndicated columnist, says contestants sometimes contrive to make their creations unique by introducing unnecessary procedures or exotic ingredients. They should submit recipes they really enjoy. Misch adds, "Ingredients should be readily accessible, both in terms of cost and availability."

Helen McCully, food editor of a leading home and food magazine, believes that the end result is often not the same as the contestant's description. Experts can often tell just by looking at recipes whether or not they are going to work. Sometimes there is a better way of achieving the desired result than the given one. Whatever the method, it should be clearly and explicitly communicated.

Dough Is the Name of the Game

In baking we make dough out of flour. This book illustrates how, in all of contesting, we make dough out of words—dough being that green stuff we never have enough of, these days. Countless cooking contests combine the definition of dough as in baking with the second meaning of dough (words that earn "dough" for us) to win those unbelievable awards. When we amalgamate food for thought with thought of food, we win that tremendous prize in a cooking contest.

Whether you bake a bread for a prize or cook up a winning entry with words alone, the prerequisites are much the same. You have to start "cooking with gas," mentally, in order to arrive at an entry *well done*. That's how you become a *big cheese* in the prize-recipe field, and begin to *bring home the bacon* and get on the *gravy* train!

Idea Starters

In baking contests, there's no match for previous winning techniques which shed light on the subject. They stir you up to participate in them. All cooking entries are heavily spiced with prize ideas, ingredients, and words which act as thought starters. Later on we will illustrate just how to combine ideas, ingredients, and words to win those top cooking-contest prizes.

Profusion of Cooking Contests

People just like you—amateur cooking contest participants who have never won another contest of any kind—are being awarded fantastic top prizes in these contests, all the time, prizes ranging from $40,000 to thousands of other tremendous awards, frequently given by food and liquor companies as well as magazines and newspapers. Additional recipe contest sponsors are *Better Homes & Gardens,* Chex Cereal, French's, Eckrich, Knox Gelatine, Red Star Dry Yeast, Seagram's, Uncle Ben's Rice, and Weight Watchers.

Must You be an Expert?

Unlike other kinds of contests, it takes no special skill to enter and win in recipe contests. Anyone who can cook might enjoy this type of competition. You don't have to be a gourmet cook or an unusual culinary expert. If you have imagination, inventiveness, like to eat (and who doesn't?), just follow the simple steps outlined in this chapter.

How Do You Cook for Company?

If you were merely cooking for guests, you'd strive to stimulate the palates of your company with superb offerings in looks and taste appeal. As the host or hostess, you would seek time-saving shortcuts, inflation-fighting economy, and mistake-proof cooking perfection. These are exactly the qualities called for in a cooking contest entry.

What do you look for in a meal, dish, or cake at home or in a restaurant? Think about it for a while. Wouldn't appearance be the first prerequisite? After that, a sampling of the taste would win over. Right? Consequently, you can understand why appearance and taste score heavily in all cooking competitions.

If you were in charge of the kitchen, wouldn't you desire a fast and simple procedure and quick preparation time? In today's hurried living pace, who wants to stand over a hot stove for a long time, figuring out a complicated recipe? Not modern folks who enjoy freedom thanks to the magic of instant foods. To please our own palates as well as those of guests, the basic ingredients and various flavors we include should be appealing and universally popular. Exotic additives may please a few, but why chance it when a group is involved?

It's always a thrill to the host or hostess when visitors ask for the recipe they've eaten. Doesn't it mean they loved it? You bet! Therefore, we must try to stimulate interest with our recipes. When guests ask questions, and specifically ask for the ingredients and the method of making the dish, there is no greater compliment.

Last but not least, in our inflation-ridden times, shouldn't economy play an important role in what we cook or bake? I should say!

Summing Up

In short, our contribution should be visually attractive, sensuous and taste-tempting. We should not have labored over it or spent lots of money on expensive ingredients. If guests ask for seconds, you have succeeded in stimulating sufficient interest. You've made it as a good cook! You have created a work of art for the palate!

Put these sound and sage observations together, then, and you have the makings of a cooking or baking champ! When you participate in recipe contests, put your best food forward in submitting those that look and taste great, are easy and convenient to prepare. Make certain they contain popular ingredients that are easily obtainable and present good value. Select sensible foods that can be served frequently to family or friends. Whether it's an old family favorite or a newly concocted recipe, always utilize familiar everyday ingredients you have on hand or can easily obtain—for example, cheese, fish, fowl, jelly, fruit, raisins, peanuts, soups, meat, peanut butter. Of additional importance, the experts tell us, is to give complete, accurate directions, proper pan sizes, and baking time and temperature. List every ingredient with exact measurements.

Telltale Titles

As in all other contests, words can be helpers in recipe contests. It doesn't hurt to have clever "contesty" names for your contributions. Remember, of course, that a recipe name by itself will not necessarily make you a winner. You must always back up a good title with an excellent recipe.

Note these clever winning recipe-names in rhyme: *Praise Raisin Pineapple Pie* (this also has alliteration in the P sound); *Thighs for Sighs, Very Berry Cake, Quicky Sticky Buns*. Notice that the names also give you a good inkling of the recipe contents. Doubtless, the products of these recipes would also have to be delicious and have a tempting appearance, and match all the salient points described earlier. However, don't you agree that the titles must have helped to catch the judges' eyes and to stimulate their taste buds?

You don't have to rhyme your recipe names. There are other title techniques. Recipe names that are take-offs or parodies on popular expressions and songs or clever puns will help win recipe contest prizes, for example: *Orange Kiss Me Cake, Howdy Kookie Krumbles, Coming Through the Rye* (whiskey), *Berried Treasures*.

Sometimes names for recipes incorporate the ingredients and give a mental picture of what's inside. Here's a $25,000 winner in the Pillsbury Bake-Off® contest 27—*Crescent Caramel Swirl*. (Not only can you picture it, you can almost taste it!) How about *Onion Lover's Twist, Pecan Surprise Bars, Banana Crunch Cake, Spicy Apple Twists, Chocolate Cherry Bars,* and *Magic Marshmallow Crescent Puffs*? (All are Pillsbury winners.) I could go on, but I'm afraid these tempting titles are making you hungry. And that's precisely why they appealed to the judges. Titles alone don't win, of course, but a superb recipe is enhanced by an excellent name.

Spinning, Winning, and Pinning Down Recipe Prizes

There's nothing to spinning these winning entries and pinning down those recipe prizes. All you have to do is spice your endeavors with excellent ingredients, season with time-saving tips, stir with good economy and speed. Then bake with precision and serve with pride!

Chapter 18

HOW TO WIN SWEEPSTAKE CONTESTS

A contest book would not be complete without a chapter on sweepstake contests. In this type of competition, the ability to write succinct sentences, clever prose, or perfect rhyme is not necessary. Many avid fans of the write-in type of contest, described in this volume, are entering sweepstake contests for two reasons:

(1) The preponderance of this kind of contest
(2) The tremendous sizes of the prizes offered

The Big Awards

Without any special skill or aptitude, ordinary people can enjoy extraordinary good fortune in prizes of this caliber.

Andrew Skirchak, Jr. was awarded the $100,000 grand prize in Kool's Lucky Lady Sweepstakes.

Richard C. Bandura of Bellevue, Nebraska, was selected as the grand prize winner in the Colgate-Palmolive $100,000 Match-Up Sweepstakes. His prize was $100,000 in U.S. savings bonds, a $10,000 bond each year for 10 consecutive years!

Harry Epley of Michigan took home the $25,000 first prize in a World Series Candy Bar Sweepstakes, and gave his wife, Ada, all the credit because she is the avid contest participant. He claims she did all the work but used his name sticker on the entry that won. He tells her that he is delighted to remain her lucky charm.

Violet Feldmann won the grand prize of an $18,000 customized Ford van in the Denimachine Sweepstakes for Coca-Cola.

Some Noteworthy Sweepstakes

Some outstanding sweepstake contests worth special mention are the following: Mrs. Filbert's Around The World Sweepstakes offering as grand prize a 21-day trip for two around the world. The Congoleum Home Sweet Home Sweepstakes offered a $75,000 home or cash equivalent. The Stayfree $250,000 Superstakes included a super-grand prize of $20,000 in solid gold bars, coins, or cash. M & M Mars $50,000 Sweepstakes included a grand prize of $25,000. The Fresh Start Match The Rainbow Sweepstakes offered 356 prizes (all in U.S. savings bonds), including a grand prize of $25,000. The Colgate Second Chance Sweepstakes included $1,000,000 and an AMC Spirit as well as 20 other AMC Spirits unclaimed in the Colgate Winners' Circle Stakes.

Is There a Fortune in Your Future?

Can you blame contestants for wanting to share in the sweepstake fortunes being given away? Winning prizes in this type of contest requires persistence, perseverance, and a positive attitude. The vast multitude of contestants submit entries to sweepstake contests in a hit-or-miss fashion, relying solely on one random submission. They also usually fail to follow the rules, and that dooms them from the beginning. This chapter, if perused carefully and thoroughly, should strengthen your chances of winning sweepstakes contests.

Sweepstake Secrets Researched

Comparatively few entrants possess the winning knowledge divulged in these pages. The author has interviewed hundreds of sweepstake winners, researched the field completely, and checked with sponsors. Once you have digested the sweepstake secrets revealed here for the first time, you will possess a tremendous advantage over your untutored competitors—an advantage which could lead to a fortune in your future.

Hints to Heed

Most people who enter sweepstakes give little thought, if any, to the actual treatment their efforts will get on the receiving end. They may devote a lot of time, effort, and postage stamps. If they are particularly enterprising, they might use oversize envelopes, colored paper, and perhaps include some amateur artwork on the outside or inside. They may even pad the envelope with heavy cardboard. Then they sit back and daydream about enjoying expected awards. But the question that comes up most often is: Have they wasted so much time on the trivia described above that they neglected to read and heed the rules? Is such information important to you as a would-be winner? Indeed, it is! A thorough comprehension of the rules of the particular sweepstakes is of the utmost importance. If you fail to follow the rules, your colored paper or weighted envelope will not pull you through!

Why not prepare and submit your entries exactly as required to enable you to have a maximum chance to win?

Qualifiers and/or 3 × 5 cards (or Whatever Size Is Required)

Entries lacking qualifiers are eliminated without further consideration. Illegible submissions meet the same fate, as do those postmarked after the sweepstake closing date. If a particular sweepstakes calls for a #10 envelope, that's a must! Don't send an oversize one or a smaller one. If a 3 × 5 card is specified, don't send paper. If paper is mentioned, don't send a card. Occasionally a 4 × 6 paper or card is called for. Needless to say, include the exact size specified. Read and heed those rules.

Exactness Is Important

Be sure the envelope containing your entry is addressed *exactly* as directed in the contest ad or on the entry blank. If it is specified that you select a prize number and include this in the lower left-hand corner, failing to do so eliminates you immediately.

If the rules state that you are to hand-address the envelope, never type it. Never use pencil. Write clearly in ink. Of course, entries that are so poorly written as to be unreadable cannot be considered. You may type entries if hand-addressing or handwriting is not mentioned in the rules.

Importance of Postmarks

When your entries have been properly addressed, your sweepstakes have passed the first hurdle. Since sweepstakes have definite closing dates, any submissions bearing a later postmark—even a single day—will be disqualified. For example, if the rules state that entries must be postmarked by May 10, try to mail early in the day of the 10th, if not before. On the other hand, if the rules say that entries must be *received* by May 10, allow at least a week for delivery. Play safe and mail about May 3. Be sure to mail your entries in time to make the proper contest deadline.

Box Tops—Blanks—Block Letters

Now comes the essential matter of qualifiers. Almost all write-in, creative contests require you to send a proof of purchase with your entry—meaning a box top, label, or wrapper from the sponsor's product. In sweepstakes, federal laws and postal regulations prohibit a sweepstake's sponsor from demanding that you purchase the product. You may buy the product, if you like, but you have the option not to buy it. In the latter case, all you are to do is write or print in block letters the sponsor's name (usually on a 3 × 5 card or paper). These are block letters:

Block
Block

(Both of these are block letters, equally acceptable. Neatness does not count, just legibility and correct spelling of the product name.)

After you have included either the qualifier or the 3 × 5 card or paper, make certain that on another, separate card or paper, you have printed or written (as specified in the rules) your own name, address, and zip code. Occasionally, a dealer's name is called for in the rules. Don't fail to include this information.

Many people mistakenly believe that they will not win a sweepstakes unless they enclose the actual label or purchase the sponsor's merchandise. It is a fact that you can win by writing the sponsor's name in block letters on those 3 × 5 cards or papers. You need not purchase the product to win. You never increase your chances by using real qualifiers.

How Many Entries to Submit?

If you're lucky, you may win a top prize with a single submission. However, you increase your odds by sending in multiple entries. In most sweepstakes you can enter as many times as you like. Avid sweepstakes enthusiasts have been known to send in 25 to 200 entries, or more. This number depends on the time you wish to allot for preparing your entries, how much you wish to spend on envelopes, cards, paper, and postage, and how interesting the prizes are.

In a recent survey I conducted among regular sweepstakes winners, I discovered that most winners average 30 to 60 entries for every sweepstakes they enter. For example, if a sweepstakes runs for 30 to 60 days, these entrants would mail one or two entries per day. If it is a sweepstakes of shorter duration, these systematic prize pursuers would mail three or four per day. If you are a real sport, you should mail several extra entries on the last few days, including the very last one. Make certain to get them to the post office in time for the proper postmark.

A few random sweepstake contests may state in their rules: "one entry per family and/or per person." As always, follow these rules. If you were selected for a top prize, and if the rules stated only one entry allowed, you would be disqualified if you had submitted more than one.

Mistake-Proof Tips

Another suggestion recommended by consistent winners is to write (at one time) all the entries you will use during the period of a sweepstakes—a month, two weeks, or whatever. The object is to stick to one sweepstakes at a time, concentrating carefully on the exact rules involved. When you have written and filed them, you can then distribute your entries at regular intervals, as suggested before, to get your contributions into as many different mailbags as you can.

If you are really eager to win, follow a similar system for all sweepstakes. Select and sort entries into different packages for all the days they are to be mailed. Bundle them with rubber bands or clips, and include the date for mailing each packet. Vary your mailing hours. If there are two pick-up hours at your mailbox or post office, vary the time of your mailings. Sometimes mail for an a.m. pick-up, and next time for a p.m. pick-up.

Special Sweepstakes Shortcuts

1. In preparing entries in quantities, have a wet sponge available for sealing envelopes and pasting stamps on envelopes. In a stationery store, you can purchase inexpensive envelope and stamp moisteners to expedite this tedious job.

2. You can address envelopes by typewriter or by hand. Find out which method is faster for you. However, if rules state "address by

hand," only that method will be acceptable. Hand-addressing envelopes and printing the sponsor's name (in block letters) can be done while you watch TV or listen to the radio. Carry some envelopes and 3 × 5 cards with you all the time, If stuck in traffic or in a doctor's waiting room, relieve the boredom by filling in some cards.

3. To build up speed, do one step at a time. Concentrate on filling in all the 3 × 5 cards with the exact requirements, carefully noted, all at once. When you get to the envelopes, make sure of what's to be included, such as something that should be written in the left hand corner. Do these all at once so as not to lose the continuity or break the rules accidentally.

4. Save time with your own name and address. Use abbreviations. But never ever omit your zip code. Once again, be sure your handwriting or typing is glance clear and readable. This rule seems obvious. Then why do I stress it? Countless numbers of entrants continue to submit illegibly written material, only to be disqualified. On the outside of your envelope, to save time, use a rubber stamp or label for your return address (unless the rules ban it).

5. Be persistent, patient, and positive. A big-time winner in Texas claims that since she adopted the power of positive thinking, she wins several sweepstake contests a week. Enter as many current contests as you can reasonably afford, consistently and systematically. This method should pay off handsomely. Remember you can't win all the sweepstakes all the time. Conversely, you won't lose all the time either. If you better your odds by continuous quantity mailings, remembering to read and heed the rules exactly—you, too, can become a big sweepstake winner.

Process for Prize Picking

Sweepstakes winners are selected on a random basis. Because of the huge volume received, computers are usually used. The color or size of your envelope or decoration has no bearing. Computers are color blind. You may gum up the works with oversize envelopes. Many judging agencies now insist on envelopes of a certain dimension for this reason. Entries are opened after the envelopes are drawn, to check if the rules have been followed. If the entry violated the rules (for example, with a wrong size envelope, typing instead of hand addressing, or late postmark) it will be discarded.

Various judging agencies process sweepstakes, and each may employ different procedures and standards. One in particular will disqualify a 3 × 5 entry if the size is 1/8″ off. Another agency won't allow rubber stamps or address labels when rules specify to "hand print" your name and address. Play it safe and always be exact in every sweepstakes requirement.

Top winners usually have to execute affidavits of eligibility and release because they fulfill the sponsor's legal requirement. It also determines that the entrant or a member of his or her immediate family is not employed by or related to the sponsoring company, the advertising agency, or the sweepstake contest judges.

Where Do You Find Sweepstake Contests?

Now that you know the ins and outs of properly participating in sweepstake contests, you will want to keep abreast of all the sweepstakes around. You will want to subscribe to one or more of the publications devoted to sweepstakes and contests. (Refer back to Chapter 13, Sources of Success). These bulletins listed offer complete information about countless sweepstakes and contests listed according to closing dates. It would take many hours of browsing through tons of magazines to scout out all the information on your own. The subscription rates of these publications are relatively inexpensive when you consider all the legwork they are sparing you and time-saving facts they relay to you. Once you take out a subscription you will be kept abreast of every sweepstake around.

"Pep" Is the Secret Ingredient

In any contest, particularly sweepstakes, I call upon *Pep* as the real winning secret necessary for achieving success:

*P*ersistence

*E*nthusiasm

*P*ositive attitude

Now it is up to you to get busy. As you start entering sweepstakes, be *P*ersistent, *E*nthusiastic and maintain a *P*ositive attitude. You can't expect to win every contest, but if you follow the advice in these pages, which is gleaned from longtime sweepstake winners and thoroughly researched information, you've got a head start on the hobby. Remember to enter consistently. You should start winning before long. You may not win the big ones in the beginning, but it is always a thrill to win anything. One never knows when that tremendous prize will come along. Keep trying for it. It's well worth the time and postage (if you can afford both) when that big pie-in-the-sky sweepstakes prize arrives. Good luck!

Chapter 19

SPEAKING TO SPONSORS

Sponsors of successful prize contests—who are far too numerous to be named here individually—certainly need no advice from the author of this book.

To such sponsors, the writer can only express deep and earnest gratitude. They have given her and hosts of other contest fans the most fascinating hobby on earth—one that is based on the fundamental emotion of hope—and *Hope springs eternal in the human breast.*

The Hobby Built on Hope

There can be no doubt that contests hold out hope of rich rewards and a better life for millions of people whose future would otherwise appear drab, humdrum, and routine. There is a powerful, stimulating allure in the prospect of attaining sudden fame and fortune by placing first in a national contest offering huge, entrancing awards.

It matters not that the sponsor's motive for running contests is to boost his business and to make bigger profits. To the eager entrant, a contest's product is less important than its by-product—which is the hope it arouses of winning a sensational prize.

Hence, all prize seekers should be grateful—and most of them are—to the sponsors whose continuous contests serve (even if only incidentally) to nurture the entrants' eternal hope of achieving some spectacular success through this hobby which offers not only the pursuit of happiness, but the happiness of pursuit.

Pointers for Prospective Sponsors

While the author frankly admits that she has nothing but heartfelt thanks to offer long-established and widely experienced contest sponsors, her purpose in this chapter goes beyond that. Her aim here is chiefly to explain the value of well-conducted creative contests to business executives who have never before employed this effective means of sales promotion.

How Creative Contests Can Benefit Your Business

The surest way to familiarize more consumers with your product or service is to run a prize contest requiring entrants to write about that particular subject. It makes little difference whether the entry is in the form of a statement, slogan, or jingle—so long as it deals directly with your product.

The lasting value of this type of promotion has been confirmed through thousands of contests which attracted many millions of entrants. A satisfyingly large proportion of these contestants became regular customers after once testing a product in order to write about it convincingly for a possible prize.

Taking a tip from these facts, a new contest sponsor should always insist upon entries that actually describe the virtues of his product. Unquestionably, that is the best way to turn a contest tryer into a steady buyer.

Other Advantages of Prize Promotion

Increasing the sales of your product by attracting new customers is probably the greatest advantage you can expect from any contest. However, there are many other ways in which contests may benefit your business. Here are some of the purposes they can serve:

Gain attention for a newly introduced product.

Find new uses for an established product.

Assure prominent product display by dealers.

Open new territory, especially through a regional contest.

Induce consumers to visit dealers for a demonstration (if your product calls for such action).

Develop a reliable mailing list of current prospects.

Obtain a usable slogan or new name for a product.

Reveal, through keyed entry coupons, which of your advertising media pulled best.

167

Improve public relations and build good will.

Overcome seasonal sales slumps.

Offset other types of campaigns by competitors.

Mark a special occasion, such as your company's 25th anniversary—or even its first.

Announce improvements in your product.

Secure testimonials for advertising use, describing how your product benefits consumers.

Why Professional Assistance Is Advisable

To get the fullest value from a contest, while avoiding a lot of extra work, trouble, and unforeseen expenses, you should secure the services of a reputable professional contest judging company.

Such firms are employed by most commercial contest sponsors, including every one whose name is nationally recognized—which accounts in great part for the success and regular repetition of their popular prize promotions.

As a prospective contest sponsor, you would do well to follow the same procedures that have been used to such advantage in this field so far. Experienced sponsors know that there are several sound reasons for hiring a professional judging agency to handle their contests. Among these reasons are the following:

1. The sponsoring company cannot be accused of showing partiality in the selection of prize winners.
2. Any resentment that might be felt by non-winners would be directed against the judging organization rather than the sponsor.
3. Reputable judging companies are insured to cover mistakes or claims of any kind likely to arise.
4. Neither sponsors nor their advertising agencies are equipped to handle the overwhelming flood of mailed entries—often numbering more than a million separate pieces—drawn by a big contest.
5. Even if all contest mail could be physically handled by the sponsor's own staff, they lack the proper qualifications to evaluate entries according to the strict standards set by post office regulations.

6. A professional judging organization can help the sponsor plan a contest from its very inception, taking into consideration any particular merchandising problems.
7. The specially trained staff of a professional judging service provides competent evaluation of all entries on an objective, impersonal basis, assuring absolute fairness to all contestants.
8. Expert appraisal of entries by qualified judges will eliminate errors in selection which could prove costly and embarrassing.
9. From long experience a professional judging organization knows how to handle legitimate queries or complaints from entrants, as well as the crank mail which some contests occasionally evoke.

A Last Word to Likely Sponsors

If you have never before conducted a contest to improve your business, increase your sales and impress the public, *now* is the time to try this profitable form of promotion, when you can call upon so many special services to assist you in creating contest themes, working up prize structures, receiving and judging entries, selecting winners, and distributing awards.

Chapter 20

PRIZE PROBLEMS AND ANSWERS

What questions about contesting came to your mind as you read through this book? There is a good chance that you will find your individual prize problems—or at least something closely akin to them—discussed in this concluding chapter.

From long experience in answering queries from readers of contest features in various magazines, the author has become familiar with the questions that seem to perplex most prize seekers. These standard inquiries, along with others that relate to special phases of the contest hobby, will be answered here.

Q. In a limerick or jingle contest, should I submit only my last line or copy the given lines and add my own?

A. If you use your own paper instead of an entry blank, it is better to copy the whole verse, adding your line about an inch or two below the other lines to make your entry stand out. Then leave more clear space under your line before filling in your name and address, and any dealer information that may be required.

Q. Some entry blanks say "write" your name, others say "sign" or "print." What's the difference?

A. The difference can be between getting a prize or not, since *rules must be followed exactly*. When asked to "write" or "sign" your name, your actual signature in longhand is wanted. "Print" means lettering either by hand or with a typewriter. For writing or printing, a pen is always preferable to a pencil. Even when typing, it's a good idea to SIGN your name by hand, to give your entry a personal touch.

Q. Are contractions like "isn't" or "she'll" considered as one word or two by contest judges?

A. While some published winning entries indicate that judges are not too strict on this point, *it is safer to count contractions as TWO words,* which they really are.

Q. May I send more than one entry to any contest?

A. If the rules do not definitely limit you to one entry, you may submit as many entries as you wish, provided each one is accompanied by whatever proof-of-purchase qualifiers may be required. However, it is better to use a separate envelope for each entry, instead of putting several in the same envelope.

Q. When rules allow the use of either entry blanks or plain paper, which is preferable?

A. If the entry blank is crowded with printed matter and limited in writing space, plain paper would let you present your entry more neatly and attractively.

Q. What should I do when in doubt as to what part of a box is the actual top, since the product name does not always appear there?

A. Send the entire front, back or side of the box along with the opening flap, so there can be no mistake about it.

Q. When contest rules say all entries become the sponsor's property, does it mean we cannot even use our non-winners again?

A. That rule has no such significance. Sponsors use the phrase "all entries become our property" to avoid demands for return of material that failed to win—not to prevent you from using the same entries elsewhere. That's why you should always keep copies of whatever you submit to a contest—*a good idea that once was a flopper may next time be a topper!*

Q. When told to "enclose" a box top or label, should I clip, staple, or paste it to my entry?

A. *Never paste or staple* the qualifier to your entry, which could easily be torn or damaged by its removal. A clip may be used, but it must be kept away from the upper part of your envelope, to avoid damage during cancellation at the post office. Your safest procedure is to enclose the qualifier loosely, without any attachment to your entry.

Q. I've noticed that addresses for the same contest are given differently in newspaper ads, magazine ads, and entry blanks. Which address should I use?

A. It doesn't really matter, since all entries for a specific contest will reach the same judging destination, regardless of minor variations in address. Different box numbers or initials are used only to let the sponsor know where his contest ads were seen.

Q. In a daily contest, may I repeat the same entry on different days?

A. Certainly. If you have composed what you consider a good entry, it's worth trying several times when non-winning entries are discarded after each day's judging is over. Remember, though, that this applies *only* to contests which award prizes on a daily, weekly, or monthly basis. For contests having but one definite closing date, you should never repeat the same entry—since *duplicated material cannot win.*

Q. Would joining a contest club help me to win more prizes?

A. Possibly. Many people succeed in winning consistently without ever joining any contest clubs. Yet others derive great benefit from social contact with fellow contestants. There's a lot of fun in sharing the same hobby with friends. By exchanging contest news and information, you may find such contacts profitable as well as pleasant.

Q. Is it O.K. to use slang words in entries?

A. If appropriate to the subject, there should be no objection; but avoid using any questionable term, like the entrant who tried to praise a girdle by saying it could be removed easily by a "short yank or a little jerk."

Q. When submitting statement entries on plain paper, should I include the starting phrase given by the sponsor?

A. Yes, this is definitely desirable, since your entry must form a complete sentence in conjunction with its beginning. However, the starting phrase does NOT count in the total number of words allowed.

Q. If I win a prize after sending several entries to a contest, is there any way I can learn which one of my entries won?

A. Usually, such information will not be disclosed by the sponsor, no matter how nicely you may ask for it. But you can "key" your entries to reveal which won by signing your name in slightly different ways on each entry submitted—as: Mary Brown, Mary J. Brown. Mrs. John Brown, Mrs. J. C. Brown, Mary Jane Brown and so on. Then, when a prize notification comes your way, you can check its name style against your keyed entry copies to identify the actual winner.

Q. When submitting opinion-type questions to TV or radio programs, should I include some kind words for the sponsoring product?

A. Better not. Such prize offers are made only to get usable material. Additional remarks are unnecessary and might even spoil your chances of winning if the judges felt that you were just trying to curry favor with your praise.

Q. What is meant by a "restricted entry"?

A. If contest sponsors do not want winning entries revealed for publication, they may require winners to withhold that information. Under such conditions, entries are said to be "restricted." In some cases, only major prize winning entries are barred from disclosure. However, many sponsors make no restrictions of any sort even on entries that have won top awards.

Q. In naming contests, are duplicated entries always discarded?

A. They would be if the contest called for a name alone. However, if an explanatory statement is required, duplicated names may win according to the merit of the accompanying reasons.

Q. Some contests ask for entries on postal cards. Would it be all right to enclose such card entries in envelopes for mailing, to keep them from being soiled by handling while in transit?

A. When rules require entries to be submitted on postal cards, anything submitted to the contest address in an envelope may be thrown away unopened and unread, since it would be considered a violation of the rules.

Q What can be done when entry blanks are necessary but not available from dealers?

A. In that case, the only thing to do is to write directly to the sponsor of the contest, explain the situation, and ask for a few blanks by mail. *Be sure to provide a stamped envelope addressed to yourself,* with your request. You can always find the sponsor's address on the contest product.

Q. In statement contests calling for "25 words or less," how much "less" would be acceptable to the judges?

A. Generally, you should try to utilize most of the words allowed—not going below fifteen at least, or it may seem that you don't have enough good things to say about the product. However, an exceptionally clever idea might be expressed best in very few words; and such brevity may impress the judges favorably once in a while.

Q. Does it ever help to send in fancy or decorated entries? If so, how can it be done best?

A. There is no use wasting your time and effort to decorate entries in national contests, where ornamentation means nothing.

In *local* contests, though, which are generally handled by nonprofessional judges, some appropriate embellishment of your entry might tip the balance in your favor after all other factors have been evaluated. Decoration is usually done by illustrating entries with cartoons or sketches to fit their subject matter.

Contestants who lack artistic ability for original drawings manage well enough with pictures clipped from magazines, comic sections, and similar sources. It would be advisable to start a file of such cut-outs under various headings like sports, children, couples, landmarks, home scenes, transportation, and many others likely to prove useful. Then, when a *local* contest is announced for which you consider decoration suitable, just pick an appropriate picture from your collection and work it into your entry.

You may even find that your "art gallery" will serve to stimulate new ideas and help you create something really unusual— which is the way to win.

Q. When a dealer's name is requested on a contest blank, does that mean the name of the store, the owner, or the clerk?

A. If the owner's name is part of the store name—like Greenbaum's Grocery—use it in just that form. If the store has an impersonal title, such as Thrifty Market, use that *plus* the name of the owner, manager, or clerk who filled your order.

Q. Would I have to pay income tax on any prize I won in a contest, even if it isn't in cash?

A. Yes. To quote from a recently published statement from the Internal Revenue Service: "Prizes and awards are generally taxable and the fair market value must be included in gross income on tax returns. Prizes and awards which are reportable include, but are not limited to, amounts received from radio and television giveaway shows, contests, door prizes, raffles, lotteries, and sweepstakes. Prizes and awards such as shares of stock, building lots, merchandise, and vacation trips are taxable. The fair market value of the trips, service, or merchandise received is the amount to be included as taxable income. This is also applicable if the recipient disposes of any such item by gift or otherwise."

Q. How can I determine what tax—if any—is due on a vacation prize, which actually cost me money to take?

A. For advice on any specific federal income tax problem, you should communicate with the Internal Revenue Service office for your district. Only an official ruling can show you the proper procedure to follow in reporting any particular kind of prize contest winnings.

Q. Is the average commercial contest completely fair and honest?

A. All contests conducted *through the mail*—which would include every one involving any form of written entry—must conform to post office regulations which govern their judging standards and procedure. That's the best insurance of their integrity. Even aside from this official controlling factor, no commercial firm would risk its reputation by sponsoring any questionable form of promotion. Contests *must* be fair and honest to serve their prime purpose of benefiting the sponsor's business.

Q. Are there any continuous contests, open for entries at any time?

A. Yes, there are competitions which run regularly and offer good money for a few words or sentences. These literary contests are covered completely and thoroughly in GLASSER GUIDE TO FILLER WRITING (See Chapter 13, Sources of Success.) You will find such continuous cash offers in every issue of *The Reader's Digest, Catholic Digest, Playboy, The National Enquirer, Family Circle, Woman's Day* and many other daily, weekly, or monthly publications. Most of these offers are made for epigrams, anecdotes, light verse, jokes, household hints, or questions, with payments ranging from $10 to $100 for each acceptable item. In addition, there is a byline and national recognition gained by the contributor. While no national commercial contest is run continuously, the same sort of competition may be conducted annually—like the contest run by *The Writer's Digest* every year. (See Chapter 13, Sources of Success.) Cooking and baking contests that are held regularly are the Pillsbury Bake-Off® Competitions, and the National Chicken Cooking

Contest. (See How to Win Recipe Contests, Chapter 17.) Other repeaters have been sponsored by: Mifflin Alcohol, FTD Florists, *Redbook*, and others, at irregular intervals.

Q. When it is announced that a contest will close on a certain date, does it mean entries must be received by that time or postmarked not later than the given date?

A. If rules are not clear on the point, always *play safe* and consider them to mean that your entries should be *received* by the date mentioned—which, in turn, means mailing them a few days before the deadline.

Q. Are the courses offered by correspondence schools worth what they charge?

A. It all depends on *your* ability to apply the teachings, which have proved sound and effective in countless contests and writing competitions. Many students claim to have won substantial sums and achieved literary acclaim from these home study lessons. To determine the potential value of these courses for yourself, write for free details to the directors of these writing schools, enclosing a *stamped, self-addressed envelope.*

> Selma B. Glasser
> c/o GLASSER GUIDE TO FILLER WRITING
> 241 Dahill Road
> Brooklyn, NY 11218

> Howard E. Doerr
> c/o Shepherd School
> P. O. Box 366
> Willingboro, NJ 08046

Q. I live on a farm a long way from any city having a contest club; yet I'd like to keep in touch with other contesters. Is there a way I can do so?

A. Yes—through a series of Round Robin letters conducted for contest fans by Ruth Roberts, 408 La Coeur Drive, La Place, LA 70068. Send her a *stamped, self-addressed envelope* for further information on this correspondence club.

Q. Is it possible to make a living entirely from prize winning, by entering every contest in a businesslike way?

A. *Absolutely not!* It would be the height of folly to expect any such result. Contesting is a hobby, not a job. Whatever prizes come your way are only a welcome supplement to your own or your family's usual source of support, generally providing more pleasure than profit. True, you *may* win a wad of cash equal to several years' normal earnings—or a car, home or vacation that you couldn't afford otherwise. But you cannot count on that possibility as a substitute for a steady salary or regular income.

Q. What were the largest and smallest prizes ever awarded in any kind of contests?

A. For solving a long series of puzzles and answering 720 difficult questions, Mrs. Lelia Boroughs of Beverly Hills, Calif., won $375,000—the biggest prize reported so far. The smallest award of any specific value on record was a half-cent U.S. postage stamp given to Mrs. R. C. Chamberlain of Chicago for her last line to this limerick:

> Don't scoff at a prize if it's small
> For it's better than nothing at all.
> And even a stamp
> May make you a champ . . .
> By gum, you'll lick Franklin—so scrawl!

Q. From reading winning entries, I know that punning helps land a prize, especially in limerick and title contests. Since I'm not very good at this trick, could you tell me if there is any sure-fire method for composing a pun on any subject?

A. Yes, you can easily learn how to compose a pun on any subject but the king—since the king isn't a subject. And there's a pun for you! Really, though, it isn't at all difficult. Just take any popular phrase or expression and change it slightly in sound or spelling. Consider the oft-heard remark, "Long time no see." A sailor on shore duty might comment: "Long time no SEA." A low-voiced singer could say: "Long time no C." A senorita who refuses her Latin lover might make him observe: "Long time no *SI*." And when your TV set breaks down in the middle of your favorite show, you might crack: "WRONG time no see!" Get the idea? And remember Ed Wynn's classic switch: "A bun is the lowest form of wheat."

Lessons 3 and 4 of GLASSER GUIDE TO FILLER WRITING contain instructive illustrations, 250 usable expressions, 120 original examples, plus 1,000 double-meaning words.

Authoritative Advice

As a special service to readers of this book, the author will personally answer—to the best of her knowledge and ability—any reasonable question concerning creative contests in particular or the writing field in general. For a prompt reply, *please enclose a self-addressed, stamped envelope.* Send your queries directly to:

Selma B. Glasser
241 Dahill Road
Brooklyn, NY 11218

GLOSSARY OF TERMS

ACROSTIC—formation of a product's or sponsor's name by special arrangement of words in an entry. Generally, the first letter of each line, reading from top to bottom, will make up the name or other message.

ALLITERATION—use of the same starting sound in several words in one group.

ANALOGY—adaptation of words from a particular field (such as sports, music, transportation) to express an entry more effectively.

APTNESS—close adherence of an entry to the specific subject of a contest.

BALANCED PHRASE—an expression that weighs one product virtue against another, as: "Maximum worth at minimum price."

CAPTION—a phrase or sentence describing a picture or cartoon; or a remark attributed to a character therein.

COINED WORD—an artificial word or name, either wholly invented or formed by combination or alteration of ordinary words.

CONTESTANT—one who enters any competition; a contest entrant.

CONTESTER—one who makes a hobby of entering contests; a *regular* prize seeker.

COUPLET—a complete verse or stanza of two rhyming lines.

CREATIVE CONTEST—a competition based on skillful composition of written entries, not including puzzles.

DEADLINE—the closing date of any contest, for mailing or receipt of entries.

DECORATION—addition of special effects, such as artwork, color, picture paste-ups or other embellishment, to an entry.

DEVICE—a contrived expression or deliberate arrangement of words to give an entry an impressive effect.

179

EPIGRAMS—witticisms, brief quotes, definitions (humorous or pointed).

ENTRANT—anyone who submits an entry in a contest.

ENTRY—a composition submitted to a contest in compliance with its rules.

ENTRY BLANK—an official form which may be required for participation in a contest.

FACSIMILE—a copy of a qualifier (box top, label) as specified by contest rules.

FILLERS—short writing pieces which enliven pages of publications—humor, human interest, epigrams, verse, etc.

FOLLOW THROUGH—natural continuity between a contest's starting phrase or given jingle lines and the entry itself.

FORMULA—a device which may be adapted for repeated use in different contests.

GIVE-AWAY—any prize distributed by chance, through lucky drawings or random picking of winners' names from general sources.

HOMONYM—a word pronounced exactly like another, though spelled differently, like "right" and "write."

INNER RHYME—a device using two or more rhyming words within the same line.

JINGLE—any short verse, usually consisting of four lines, of which at least two must rhyme.

JUDGE—(noun) an evaluator of entries who decides upon their relative merit and final standing; (verb) to grade entries according to certain standards.

KEYING—using variations of one's name (or other signs) to identify which of several entries may prove to be a winner.

LAST LINE—the line to be added to an incomplete limerick or jingle.

LIGHT VERSE—humorous, short poetry.

LIMERICK—a verse of five lines, in which the first, second, and fifth lines rhyme with one another and the third and fourth lines rhyme with each other.

LOCAL CONTEST—a competition open only to residents of the community in which it is held.

METER—the regular rhythm or cadence of a line or verse.

NATIONAL CONTEST—a competition open to all or most of the fifty states.

ORIGINALITY—freshness or novelty of thought and expression— an important factor in evaluating entries.

PARODY—a modified version of a well-known expression, saying, title, proverb, or any famous utterance. In contest terminology, "parody" and "paraphrase" are used interchangeably.

PATTERN—same as "formula."

PERSONIFICATION—attributing human feelings, emotions, and actions to inanimate objects.

PROSE—speech or writing that is not deliberately rhymed or rhythmic.

PUN—(as a noun) a word altered for humorous or double-meaning effect; (as a verb) to make a pun.

QUALIFIER—the proof-of-purchase required with an entry, such as a box top, label, wrapper, sales receipt, etc.

QUALIFY—to validate an entry for judging consideration by accompanying it with whatever proof-of-purchase may be required.

QUATRAIN—a verse of four lines, in any rhyming order.

REGIONAL CONTEST—a competition limited to residents of a designated geographical area.

RHYME—correspondence in the sounds of two or more words, usually in the last syllable.

RHYMING DICTIONARY—a volume that groups words according to their matching terminal sounds or rhymes.

RHYTHM—regular recurrence of accented words or syllables in a line of verse.

SALES POINT—a special virtue of a product emphasized in an entry.

SLANT—(noun) planned inclination of entries to meet stated judging standards; (verb) to strive for that effect.

SLOGAN—a brief, pithy phrase describing the salient feature of a product, or urging a specific course of action.

SPONSOR—(noun) the financial backer of a contest; (verb) to provide funds for the conduct of a contest.

STANZA—a part or division of a poem, comparable to a paragraph in prose.

STATEMENT—the conclusion, in not more than 50 words, of a contest's starting phrase. A longer entry is generally called a "letter."

SWEEPSTAKES—a drawing of winners' names by pure luck or chance, in which skill plays no part.

SYNONYM—a word similar in meaning to another one.

TITLE—same as "caption," though applicable to a range of subjects wider than pictures and cartoons.

TRIAD—a device using three related items or phrases in one entry.

UNIQUENESS—the element of difference in an entry that makes it impossible to be duplicated by any other submission.

VERSE—a composition in rhymed and/or rhythmical form.

WINNERS LIST—an announcement naming all prize winners released by the sponsor upon conclusion of a contest.

WORD PLAY—contrived arrangement or alteration of words to make an entry more effective.

ZERO—rating of an entry that fails to follow most of the tips given in this book.

ABOUT THE AUTHOR

SELMA GLASSER practices what she teaches. And what she teaches is how a sense of humor, a few words and a batch of postage stamps can be combined for fun and profit. "The World's Greatest Hobby" has showered her with prizes that include trips to Rome, Paris, Puerto Rico and all over the U.S., and dinners out with Sid Caesar and Englebert Humperdinck. Frank Sinatra had her flown to the Fontainebleau Hotel in Miami for his opening night performance. For 25 well-written words she was awarded a complete gas heat and hot water system for her home. Since she took up entering contests in earnest, she has won a car, cash and lots of merchandise.

Ms. Glasser also excels in writing and selling fillers and short items —serious and funny, in prose and rhyme—to a wide range of national publications which include *Reader's Digest*, *Playboy*, *The Saturday Evening Post*, *San Francisco Examiner*, *Los Angeles Times*, *Good Housekeeping* and many others.

At Brooklyn College she teaches a course entitled: "Writing for Prize and Publication." She contributes monthly columns to *Golden Chances* and *Prizewinner*, and her "how-to-write" articles appear regularly in *The Writer* and *Writer's Digest*. Her most accomplished endeavor is a mail-order correspondence course, "Glasser Guide to Filler Writing," which incorporates her "know-how" and "show-how" and features ample samples and examples of her published writings and prize-winning words. It covers the whole gamut of filler and contest writing in 15 lessons starting with "The Write Attitude" and winding up with complete market listing opportunities. Her book *Analogy Anthology* is in its third printing.

In 1979, she served as Early Bird Chairperson for The National Contesters Association's 40th anniversary convention. She also conducts writing seminars, makes speeches and acts as Workshop Leader at the annual Philadelphia Writers' Conference. Ms. Glasser is listed in *Who's Who of American Women*, *World's Who's Who of Women* (Cambridge, England), *Who's Who Among Freelance Writers* and other prestigious publications.